The People's Budget

Dale • Eisenach • Luntz • Muris • Schneider

The People's Budget

A Common Sense Plan *for* Shrinking *the* Government *in* Washington

Regnery Publishing, Inc.
Washington, D.C.

Library of Congress Cataloging-in-Publication Data

The people's budget : a common sense plan for
shrinking the government in Washington / by Edwin L. Dale . . . [et al.] ;
with a foreward by the Honorable John Kasich.
        p.   cm.
   ISBN 0-89526-722-5
   1. Budget deficits—United States.
   2. Deficit financing—United States.
   3. United States—Economic policy—1993- I. Dale, Edwin L.
   HJ2051.P468   1995
   336.3'9'0973—dc20   95-9253
                                          CIP

Published in the United States by
Regnery Publishing, Inc.
An Eagle Publishing Company
422 First Street, SE, Suite 300
Washington, DC 20003

Distributed to the trade by
National Book Network
4720-A Boston Way
Lanham, MD 20706

Printed on acid-free paper.
Manufactured in the United States of America

10 9 8 7 6 5 4 3 2 1

Books are available in quantity for promotional or premium use. Write to Director of Special Sales, Regnery Publishing, Inc., 422 First Street, SE, Suite 300, Washington, DC 20003, for information on discounts and terms or call (202) 546-5005.

THE PEOPLE SPEAK OUT

Over the past year, Dr. Frank Luntz has traveled across the nation to listen to and learn from the wisdom and experiences of average Americans. The quotations that appear throughout this book come from more than 100 sessions he conducted over the past eight months or from "open-ended" responses to questions asked in nationwide polls.

The purpose of a focus group is to understand motivations and emotions rather than measure them. Ten or twelve individuals are gathered around a large table for two hours of serious dicussion about the past, present, and future of the country. The moderator asks each group a scrics of structured questions, but often the most poignant comments are volunteered by participants talking to each other the way neighbors do.

The following is a summary of the places and people who contributed their words, emotions, hopes, and fears to *The People's Budget:*

Location	Participants
Atlanta, GA	Baby boomers
Baltimore, MD	Perot voters/Democrats
Boston, MA	Liberals
Chicago, IL	Independents
Columbia, SC	General population
Denver, CO	Perot voters
Des Moines, IA	Low incomes
Hartford, CT	Baby boomers
Houston, TX	General population
La Crosse, WI	Women
Los Angeles, CA	Perot voters/Republicans
Nashville, TN	General population
New York, NY	Pre-retirees
Reno, NV	Conservatives
Tampa, FL	Senior citizens
Washington, DC	General population

The People's Budget

A Common Sense Plan *for* Shrinking *the* Government *in* Washington

by

★

Edwin L. Dale, Jr.
Jeffrey A. Eisenach
Frank I. Luntz
Timothy J. Muris
William Schneider, Jr.

★

With a Foreword by
the Honorable John Kasich

Edwin L. Dale, Jr.   From 1955 to 1976, Dale was an economic correspondent with the Washington and Paris Bureaus of *The New York Times*. In 1977, he joined the staff of the Subcommittee on Economic Stabilization of the House Banking Committee. During the Reagan administration, Dale was the assistant director for public affairs as well as spokesman under Directors David Stockman and James Miller at the Office of Management and Budget

(OMB). In late 1987, he became counselor to Secretary of Commerce William Verity. From there, after the election of President Bush, Dale returned to OMB, serving as counselor and director of external affairs until his retirement in 1992. ★

Jeffrey A. Eisenach Eisenach is president of The Progress & Freedom Foundation. He served two tours of duty at President Reagan's OMB and holds a Ph.D in Economics from the University of Virginia. He has served as a scholar at the American Enterprise Institute, the Heritage Foundation and the Hudson Institute, and taught economics at George Mason University and Virginia Polytechnic Institute and State University. Since 1988, he has served as a leading advisor to House Speaker Newt Gingrich. His previous books include *America's Fiscal Future: The Federal Budget's Brave New World* (Hudson Institute, 1991) ★

Frank I. Luntz Luntz is president of the Luntz Research Companies, Inc., a survey research organization. During 1992, he served as chief pollster for independent presidential candidate H. Ross Perot. The author of *Candidates, Consultants & Campaigns* (Basil-Blackwell, 1988) Luntz is also a noted scholar, serving as an adjunct professor at the University of Pennsylvania and previously on the faculty of the Graduate School of Political Management at George Washington University. Luntz received his doctorate in politics in 1987 from Oxford University. ★

Timothy J. Muris Muris is Foundation Professor of Law at the George Mason University School of Law. In the Reagan administration, he served as executive associate director of OMB, where he was responsible for overseeing preparation of the President's budget. His many publications on the budget include *The Budget Puzzle: Understanding Federal Spending* (Stanford University Press, 1994). ★

William Schneider, Jr.   Schneider is an adjunct fellow at the Indianapolis, Indiana-based Hudson Institute. During the Reagan administration, he served as the senior OMB official responsible for overseeing the defense and foreign affairs budget and later served as under secretary of State. He currently serves as chairman of the Department of State's Defense Trade Advisory Group and as a consultant to the Department of State, the Department of Defense, and the Office of Science and Technology Policy. His previous books include *Arms, Men and Military Budgets* (Transaction Press, 1976). ★

CONTENTS

CONTENTS

FOREWORD
by
Hon. John Kasich[1]

This spring, we in the Congress will begin the process of changing the government in Washington. After forty years of one-party control—an unhealthy situation no matter which party you belong to—the American people elected a new majority to the U.S. House. Our job is to do what the people asked us to do on November 8: make the government in Washington smaller, end deficit spending and balance the budget and, when we are done, produce a federal government that is strong and effective in performing its key functions.

The task before us is huge. This book details how the government in Washington has grown over the past sixty years and how far out of control things have gotten. Entitlement programs like Medicare and Medicaid are growing at 10 percent every year; discretionary spend-

[1]Congressman John Kasich represents Ohio's twelfth congressional district and serves as Chairman of the House Budget Committee.

ing—supposedly limited by "spending caps" enacted in 1990—is growing almost as fast. Literally hundreds of agencies and programs are scattered through the government that simply don't work. And when you add it all up, you have deficits year after year, deficits that have accumulated in a federal debt of nearly $5 trillion.

That debt is one of the reasons change has to occur and has to occur immediately. According to the Joint Economic Committee, a child born in 1995 will pay $187,150 *just in interest payments* on the national debt. Our children will have fewer jobs, pay higher taxes, have lower incomes, and be less able to afford homes because of the debt. By raising interest rates and discouraging investment, the debt is slowing—some would say crippling—our ability to transition into the Information Age economy of the twenty-first century.

The path we are on today is one of slow but certain erosion of America's economic strength. No economy, no matter how prosperous, can afford to pile up literally trillions upon trillions of dollars of debt.

The path we are on today is also fundamentally wrong. It used to be that parents worked hard to pay off the mortgage so they could leave the house to their children. Today, it seems, we are selling off the house and leaving the children with the mortgage. Balancing the budget is not just an economic issue. It is a moral imperative.

But the budget fight is ultimately about much more than the federal debt. It is about what kind of government we want to have in America. For the last forty years, government has taken power away from the people. The tax burden on the average American family—after adjusting for inflation—has nearly tripled, from $6,970 in 1959 to

$18,500 in 1995. Fully half of the average family's income now goes to pay taxes to federal, state, and local governments combined. As the government's budget has grown, the people's budget has shrunk.

Every time government takes a dollar from an American family, it is a dollar less that the family has to spend on feeding, educating, providing health care, and creating a safe and nurturing home for its children. It is a dollar less it has to provide for the parents' retirement or to help out grandparents.

For forty years, the government in Washington has acted as though it, not the American people, was responsible for these things. It has taken money from people to create centralized, bureaucratic programs, run by well-meaning government employees who are asked to do the impossible: design a "one-size-fits-all" government for a country of 260 million people. The simple reality is that it doesn't work and it can't work. It is a matter of common sense: no one can sit in Washington, D.C. and try to tell people in Columbus, Ohio; Austin, Texas; Abilene, Kansas; New York, New York; Detroit, Michigan; and Los Angeles, California the best way to educate children, house the poor, build the roads, and do the literally thousands of other things now dictated from Washington.

The new majority in the House will produce a budget to completely transform the government in Washington. I do not endorse every proposal listed in this book, but I have no doubts about its basic thrust. We will:

★ End the myth of federal compassion by sending responsibility for welfare programs back to the states, the localities, and the people;

★ Reform the Pentagon to make it more efficient, and revi-
talize America's defenses and cut foreign aid;

★ Cut subsidies to the hundreds of special interests—the
privileged, the powerful, and the elite—who have fed for
too long at the federal trough;

★ Send control over dozens of government activities back
to the states, restoring the spirit of the Tenth Amendment
of the Constitution; and

★ Save the Medicare system from bankruptcy by transforming it into a 21st century system of consumer choice
and quality health care.

And when we are done we will have a smaller government, lower taxes, and a balanced budget.

The government we create will also be far stronger
and more effective than the government we have today.
The distinction here, between size and strength, is crucial
to understanding everything this transformation is about.
A strong government would have a clarity of purpose, a
sense of mission and a dedication to success the current
federal government lacks. What we have today is a government that is large, but not purposeful. It is scattered
and, in most things it does, ineffective.

The government we will work to create—in the
budget we will write this year and through a long-range
process that may take a decade—is a lean but strong
government. A government that spends no more than it
takes in, that does well those essential things it should
do, and that keeps its word. We will work to create a government that works every day to earn the trust of the
people.

Trust also has to go in the other direction—the government has to trust the people. In his famous nineteenth-

century book, *Democracy in America*, Alexis de Tocqueville wrote:

> I must say that I have seen Americans make great and real sacrifices to the public welfare; and I have remarked a hundred instances in which they hardly ever failed to lend faithful support for each other. The fee institutions which the inhabitants of the United States possess, and the political rights of which they make so much use remind every citizen, and in a thousand ways, that he lives in society. . . . every instant impresses upon his mind the notion that it is the duty, as well as the interest, of men to make themselves useful to their fellow-creatures.

For too many years, the government in Washington has acted as though there was something wrong with the American people, something that could be fixed if Washington would only spend enough money, create enough programs, hire enough bureaucrats, and pass enough laws to make the people better.

Changing that attitude, that condescending notion that "Washington knows best," is what the coming transformation is all about. Before the people can trust their government again, the government is going to have to trust the people.

In that context, *The People's Budget* is a unique and important book. Before getting out their computers and their budget charts, the authors of this book asked a question most "budget wonks" never even think of: What kind of government do the people want?

The People's Budget proposes a budget for the American people. As Chairman of the House Budget Committee, I appreciate its thoroughness, its attention to detail, its reliance on conservative assumptions. Those things are all important as we move forward to craft a budget. But I suspect most readers will appreciate something else: its freshness and its common sense approach.

The new era that began in 1994 will evolve over many years. This book and the work we will be doing in Congress this year are only a first step. But we will transform the government in Washington, and to do that we need a vision, firmly rooted in the wisdom of the American people. This book is it. ★

The People's Budget

CHAPTER ONE

A People's Budget

The election in November 1994 was more than a victory of one political party over another. It was the last election of an old era and the first election of a new one.

The old era began sixty-two years earlier, with the election of Franklin Roosevelt and the start of the New Deal. Its defining characteristic was the growth of the power and size of the federal government.

★ Federal government spending as a percentage of national output increased from 8 percent of the gross domestic product in 1932 to over 24 percent in 1983 and now hovers at 22 to 23 percent. [See Figure 1.1]

★ The top income tax rate rose from 25 percent in 1931 to a peak of 90 percent.

★ The number of cabinet-level departments increased from nine to fifteen.

★ The federal debt rose from $19.5 billion in 1932 to $3.5 trillion today.

Figure 1.1

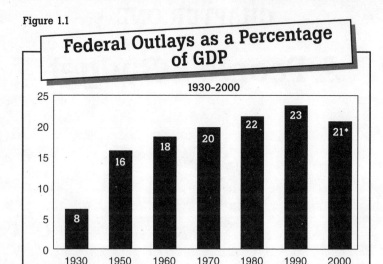

The New Deal was about much more than numbers. It was about power. New Deal theorists such as Arthur Schlesinger and John Kenneth Galbraith believed in a theory of power known as "bureaucracy." Developed by German social architect Max Weber, this system came along just in time to allow Otto von Bismarck, the great German statesman and social reformer, to implement his plans for a "Social Welfare State"—the first serious effort to create a "social safety net" on a national scale.

Bureaucracy was imported to America by progressives from both American political parties—from Theodore Roosevelt and Herbert Hoover. Bureaucracy would replace the corrupt politics of patronage—especially dominant in America's big cities and in state governments—with enlightened "scientific" government. Civil servants—smart, well-educated, impartial managers—would apply the best knowledge and the best tools to make government work better for everyone.

Modern critics of the New Deal sometimes forget how much America accomplished using this bureaucratic model of centralized power. From Normandy to the North Atlantic Treaty Organization (NATO), from the interstate highway system to rural electrification, from the power of General Motors to the productivity of IBM, from the Manhattan Project that created the atomic bomb to NASA's landing on the moon, the bureaucratic system brought America success after success.

Beginning in the 1960s, however, things started going wrong. The first problem came when the federal government plunged into areas in which it simply did not belong. President Lyndon Johnson's Society vastly expanded the bureaucratic state, promising a massive War on Poverty that would apply to America's social problems the same kind of disciplined, scientific approach that had worked in World War

> **"B**ureaucracies don't solve problems. If they did, the bureaucrats would all be out of jobs."

II. In the 1970s, President Richard Nixon presided over a dramatic expansion of federal regulations that created agencies like the Environmental Protection Agency and the Occupational Safety and Health Administration. And although President Carter campaigned as a reformer and in some areas actually tried to reduce the role of the federal government (for example, deregulating air fares and abolishing the Civil Aeronautics Board), the power of the federal government continued to grow. By the end of the 1970s, the federal government had grown in size and power beyond anything Franklin Roosevelt could have imagined. [See Figure 1.2]

Moreover, at the very time the role of the federal bureaucracy was expanding, other areas of society were beginning to learn that large, centralized bureaucracies were no longer an efficient way of getting things done. The American auto companies were perhaps the first to learn this lesson when the oil crisis of the 1970s gave the Japanese a major opening into the American market. America's Big Three (Chrysler, Ford, and General Motors) assumed that when oil prices dropped, things would get back to "normal." They were surprised to learn that, in the meantime, the Japanese—following the teachings of American management guru W. Edwards Deming, who emphasized decentralized work teams and quality—had learned to make better cars at lower prices.

At the same time, the "information revolution" began transforming the economy: big was no longer better.

Figure 1.2

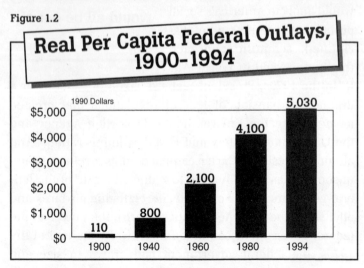

Real Per Capita Federal Outlays, 1900-1994

Anyone with a personal computer could do most of the things large bureaucracies used to do—and do them faster and better. Partly as a result, about two-thirds of the net new jobs created in America since 1970 have been created by small, growing businesses.

The transformation from "big is better" to "small is beautiful" has now taken place in almost every facet of American life—save one: the federal government. Indeed, the government is so tardy in learning this lesson that it continues, on occasion, to try to usurp even more power. But with a difference. Lately, it has found the people singularly unsympathetic with its designs. In 1989, for example, Congress passed the Catastrophic Health Care Act, a vast expansion of the Medicare program. One year later, after widespread public outcry, the very same people who passed the bill were forced to repeal it.

> **"Government is too big. If it continues to get bigger, it will crowd out people's ability to achieve the American Dream. We have to make it smaller—do the things that really count—and let the people do the rest for themselves."**

And then there was President Clinton's ill-fated proposal for a bureaucratically dominated makeover of the health care system. Inside the Beltway, all the experts expected the plan to be adopted—but it was so unpopular with the voters that Congress never even voted on it.

Since at least 1976—for nearly twenty years—American voters have tried to elect presidents who would "reform" and "cut" the bureaucracy. President Carter campaigned as a reformer who would apply "zero-based-budgeting." President Reagan promised to cut taxes and regulations. President Bush campaigned in 1988 as Reagan's successor, promising to carry on the "revolution" that had begun in 1980; when he failed, Americans turned reluctantly to President Clinton—who promised to cut taxes and "end welfare as we know it."

> "It's not the politicians we should blame. It's ourselves, because we don't have the guts enough to make the change."

As Americans watched the failures of each successive reform effort, they grew increasingly frustrated. In 1976, according to a CBS/*New York Times* survey, just over one-third of Americans (34 percent) trusted the government in Washington to do what was right "just about always" or "most of the time." By 1993, their confidence had slipped to less than one-quarter (24 percent).

On Wednesday, November 9, 1994, the day after the election, Luntz Research surveyed over 1,200 Americans to find out what they were thinking as they went to the polls. The results were stunning. Two-thirds (66 percent) had come to think of Washington as so out of touch that it could properly be referred to as an "Imperial City."

The survey asked directly about the size and power of the federal government. Nearly three out of four (73 percent) said "the federal government is much too large and has too much power." [See Figure 1.3] Every single voter group agreed with this statement by a wide margin. And

Figure 1.3

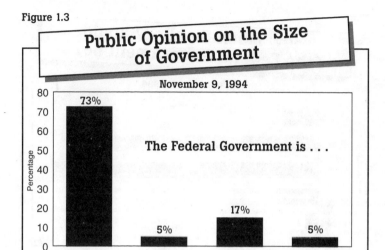

Public Opinion on the Size of Government

November 9, 1994

The Federal Government is . . .

Too Big: 73%
Too Small: 5%
About Right Size: 17%
No Opinion: 5%

Source: The Progress & Freedom Foundation & Luntz Research

when asked how much smaller the government should get, nearly half (47 percent) said it should shrink in size and power by 30 percent or more, and more than two out of three (60 percent) said it should shrink by at least 20 percent. [See Figure 1.4]

Thus, it was hardly surprising when, in the middle of the battle over the House Republicans' plans to increase spending on school lunches by 4.5 percent a year (the Democrats said this was too little and called it a "cut"), Americans—by a 3-1 ratio—told the *Los Angeles Times* that the Republicans were not cutting enough!

America's founding fathers recognized that the people would often be "ahead of" their elected officials. It remains unclear whether this new generation of leaders, this "new majority," will move quickly enough to bring about the needed downsizing of government. But the peo-

Figure 1.4

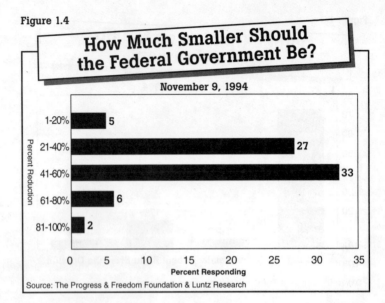

How Much Smaller Should the Federal Government Be?

November 9, 1994

Source: The Progress & Freedom Foundation & Luntz Research

ple are persistent, and their budget—the People's Budget—will be enacted.

The New Deal is ancient history. The centralized, bureaucratic system of power it was based on has died in institution after institution—from General Motors to IBM to the Soviet Union. But in America's federal government, it lives on. Federal spending is a measure of its size; the federal deficit is a measure of how dysfunctional it has become.

Can anything be done about it? The answer is yes. That is what this book is all about.

A RADICAL PLAN

Although it sounds like a contradiction in terms, success in the "conservative" revolution that began with the congressional elections of 1994 requires a large dose of the "radical."

But radical in an unfamiliar sense of the word. It is certainly not "radical left," and it is not "radical right." Instead it is radical in the sense of willingness to challenge long-accepted ideas and ways of doing things. That is, it is radical by the standards of Washington, D.C.

Everywhere else in America, the People's Budget will be recognized by a different name: common sense. Indeed, it is remarkable how, when held up against what makes sense to the American people, all kinds of seemingly sacrosanct Washington government activities do not make any sense—even though many of them had a worthy purpose when they began. Americans need to ask the following questions:

★ Do paid bureaucrats in Washington, D.C., know better than the citizens of individual cities, towns, and counties how to provide help to the poor? Common sense says they do not. In Washington, the idea of turning welfare back to the states is "radical."

★ Should special interest groups—from corporations to labor unions, farmers to artists—receive billions of dollars solely because they possess the political power to get them? Common sense says no. In Washington, to go against the special interests is considered "radical."

★ Should programs that have been tried for twenty years or more in such areas as job training and education and have a record of failure be allowed to continue? Common sense says no. In Washington, it is "radical" to terminate any program that sounds as if it were intended to help children or the poor.

★ Should Medicare be allowed to race toward bankruptcy, when we know how to modernize and transform the system to provide more choices for senior citizens at a lower cost to everyone? Common sense says no. In Washington, real changes in Medicare are considered "radical."

★ Should a bureaucratic government designed in the 1930s, a government that Americans believe is the biggest single threat to the country's future progress, that levies taxes so heavy that they kill opportunity and destroy jobs, that runs a deficit so high it squeezes out private sector investment—continue unchanged? Washington's answer is that fundamental change is "too radical." The people's answer, we believe, is that fundamental change is nothing more than common sense.

Figure 1.5

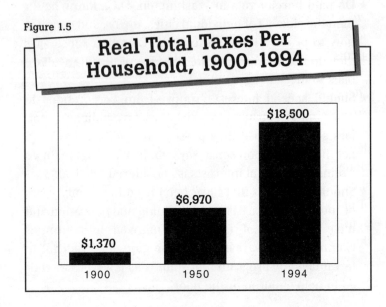

Real Total Taxes Per Household, 1900–1994

$18,500

$6,970

$1,370

1900   1950   1994

Fortunately for those who may be meek or timid or "moderate," conservative radicalism has a weapon of compelling force: the proposed constitutional amendment that would require the federal government to balance its budget by the year 2002. The new majority in Congress says this will be done by reducing spending, not raising taxes, and that it will be done whether or not the constitutional amendment clears Congress and goes to the states.

To achieve balance by 2002, government must be *transformed*. Many programs and even entire cabinet departments must be abolished. For other programs, now growing at 10 percent a year or more, the growth rate must be reduced to a sustainable level. Such changes will not come easily.

Yet as we looked hard at the federal government and what it does, we made a remarkable discovery. *With entirely reasonable, common sense changes, the federal budget can be balanced in 2002 at a lower level of taxes than we now have.* That is, the nation can cut enough federal spending to eliminate the deficit and cut taxes.

This book proposes a full-fledged budget. We call it *The People's Budget* for two reasons: The people last November signaled that the role of Washington should be sharply changed and reduced. And this plan will bring decision-making closer to the people themselves—to individuals, families, neighborhoods, local governments, and state governments, in that order. We offer not merely a list of proposed spending cuts. What we have done, with the help of many people, is to develop a full-fledged budget for the United States government—a complete blueprint for downsizing and transforming the government in Washington into a smaller, more modern, less intrusive, more effective, and much less expensive institution. The numbers and the economic assumptions add up—they add up to less money for the government and more money for the people!

In developing our proposals, we put every major program in the federal budget to a seven-part test:

> **"We've got to turn a lot of power back to the states and let them run their own governments. We've got to let them run the show for a while."**

1. Does the program or activity serve a broad national interest, or does it only subsidize some politically powerful interest group with an appealing argument, at the cost of the American people? This question applies not only to spending programs but also to special provisions of the tax law.

2. Has the program worked? Has it met its objectives? Many of Washington's "social programs," for example, have simply failed—a judgment reached by objective observers only after several decades of failure. Foreign aid programs to aid the economic development of the poorer countries are another good example.

3. Is a benefit program, although warranted, too generous because of the political clout of the group being benefited? This question applies to several of the big entitlement programs.

4. In the case of federal aid to local programs and projects, would these programs be deemed urgent by the locals even if the feds were not picking up the tab? We have looked with a skeptical eye at the whole panoply of

federal grants in aid to the states, which make programs
appear to be "free" to the local citizens when of course
they are not. Too many programs are undertaken not
because the community needs them but simply because
the federal government is willing to pay for them.

5. Can private, for-profit business achieve the same
goal or perform the same service as well as or better than
the government?

6. If a government solution is necessary, can the
objective be met at the state or local level, without the
deadening uniformity imposed by Washington?
Decentralized approaches respect the nation's diversity
and encourage experimentation.

7. Where there is a national consensus that a program should be retained but, as with Medicare or the
Earned Income Tax Credit, it is growing at an unsustainable pace, how can the growth be slowed while retaining
the essence of the program?

What remains when these seven tests are applied is a
strong, effective, and very substantial government: a
strong national defense, effective law enforcement for federal crimes, necessary regulation for national markets,
Social Security and Medicare for the elderly, institutions
needed for maintaining the currency and conducting foreign relations—and, unavoidably, a mechanism for collecting the taxes needed to pay for all these activities.

But the amount that will be collected in federal taxes
will be smaller and the huge budget deficit will be eliminated. And what is left for the American people—the real
people's budget—is much larger than if the changes we
propose here had not been enacted.

We have grouped our proposals into five areas.

First, we show how the whole panoply of welfare programs can and should cease to be a federal responsibility and be shifted instead to the states and local governments and private charities. This change is suggested not just to save money, but because state and local governments are much more likely to find solutions to the poverty problem and its accompanying social pathologies if freed from the deadening constraints of distantly imposed federal rule.

The end of federal responsibility for welfare does not mean abandoning the poor. It means what it says—the end of *federal* involvement, which has brought us failure. And it does not mean bankrupting the states. The states would have total flexibility to deal with the poor and could tap revenue resources given up by the federal government in exchange. For example, we specifically propose ending all federal excise taxes—on gasoline, alcohol, telephones, and even tobacco—to provide the states with the tax base from which to raise new revenues. Nor, however, would this arrangement amount to a mere shift of spending from the federal government to the states. There would be a substantial net savings and state agencies (forbidden, unlike the feds, to run a deficit) would be able to search out new and more efficient ways to bring help to the truly needy.

We believe, as do most Americans, that the nation has a far better chance of finding a solution to the deeply discouraging welfare problem—with its tragic impact on generation after generation of American children—by allowing the states to experiment freely than by continuing to try to "reform" the system through uniform, nationwide requirements and regulations from the distant government in Washington.

This brand new approach to welfare would be the largest single source of reduced federal spending. Its details are spelled out in Chapter Three, "Ending the Myth of Federal Compassion," where we also propose significant reforms in the Earned Income Tax Credit and in subsidized housing programs for the poor and introduce a new element in the approach to poverty—a tax credit for gifts to charitable organizations that help low-income people in the areas of health, education, and welfare.

Next we turn to defense. While we believe most Americans want a strong defense, it is also clear that the Defense Department has become top-heavy, bureaucratic, and grossly inefficient. In Chapter Seven, we offer proposals that would fundamentally transform the defense establishment—to force it to make the kinds of changes most American companies have already made by shifting to a less bureaucratic, more efficient way of doing business. We also propose an end to the use of the defense appropriations bill as a hidden source of funds for such nondefense purposes as medical research and earmarked grants to universities. The result of all our changes would be an even stronger defense—a sound defense posture cannot and should not be sacrificed to achieve budget savings— but also substantial savings: an actual reduction in defense spending over the next five years, with a return to modest growth only after the downsizing is complete. We believe—as do most Americans—that a fat defense establishment is not necessarily a strong one.

Chapter Seven also discusses foreign assistance and the international affairs bureaucracy. Foreign aid is all too often a form of international welfare, and this form of welfare causes many of the same problems as our domestic

welfare programs. Every time we subsidize a failed, inefficient project in some foreign land, we are slowing its
progress. In the process, we create dependency and
destroy initiative. While foreign aid is a relatively small
part of the federal budget (roughly $22 billion out of a bud-
get of $1.5 trillion), it is perhaps the one item Americans
most want to see cut. And they are right. We would cut it
by nearly one-third by the end of the century.

Another form of government spending Americans
have lost patience with is spending to benefit special interests. In Chapter Four, "Cutting Subsidies to the Privileged,
the Powerful, and the Elite," we propose reductions or terminations of a wide variety of federal subsidies. Our targets are not just the rich, but any group that uses political
power and privilege to get special treatment at the
expense of the taxpayers— including corporations, farmers, labor unions, veterans, and elite groups such as those
that benefit from the Corporation for Public Broadcasting
and the National Endowment for the Arts.

Next, in a chapter entitled "Sending It Home:
Restoring the Tenth Amendment," we propose combining
a host of current federal programs of grants to the states in
such areas as education and job training into interim block
grants and eventually ending altogether most federal
spending in these areas. We take a critical look at the very
concept of grants to the states—which makes various programs seem "free" when they are not. We show how
numerous federal programs designed to provide job training, for example, have been all but complete failures. The
time has come to face that reality.

Then we address the crisis in Medicare, the massive
program that provides health care for America's elderly.

Figure 1.6

The People's Budget

($ in Billions)				
	1995	**1998**	**2000**	**2002**
Revenue as % of GDP	19.3	18.6	15.7	15.9
Outlays as % of GDP	21.8	19.7	16.2	15.7
Revenues	1355	1521	1416	1577
Outlays–Discretionary				
Defense	270	264	266	277
Non-Defense	279	224	193	196
Total Discretionary Outlays	548	489	458	473
Outlays–Mandatory				
Social Security	334	385	424	467
Medicare	178	205	236	274
Medicaid	89	109	0	0
Other	226	234	166	169
Total Mandatory Outlays	827	932	825	911
Offsetting Receipts	-80	-81	-89	-96
Net Interest	235	265	270	269
Outlays	1530	1604	1464	1555
Surplus (Deficit)	-175	-83	-48	22
Memorandum–Deficit with Interest Dividend	-175	-73	-22	50

[1]Numbers may not add due to rounding.

We propose a major reform of Medicare, while retaining the entitlement of the elderly and disabled to federal health insurance. Medicare is the third largest federal program behind Social Security and defense, and for years it has been growing much faster than inflation or than the budget at large. The major part of Medicare is funded by a trust fund that will soon be bankrupt. There is virtually no hope either of saving Medicare or of balancing the federal budget without reforms to slow Medicare's spending growth significantly.

Strikingly, the rapid growth of Medicare—to more than $170 billion of outlays this year—does not stem mainly from the growth in the number of beneficiaries or from medical care inflation, though both of those contribute. The main villain is *greater utilization of medical services* by the beneficiaries. There is no reason to suppose that today's 70-year-olds are sicker than yesterday's, but they are certainly using doctors and hospitals more intensively. Part of the problem is that doctors and hospitals, complaining about allegedly niggardly Medicare reimbursement rates, have learned to play the system: by giving more and more tests and treatment, they can increase their incomes.

Cost control strategies up to now have depended on controls, and they haven't worked. As we will see, the supposed "cuts" in Medicare made by Congress year after year have been largely phony, as evidenced by the continued extremely rapid growth of spending on the program. But Congress has given the health providers a powerful argument that the "cuts" have been at the health care providers' expense. Their tears are often crocodile tears, but Congress listens.

Medicare *can* be modernized and transformed, and the private health care sector is already showing the way. A major element in the transformation will be to increase choices in Medicare. Beneficiaries will be able to choose between the current system and new options, including Medical Security Accounts with catastrophic insurance coverage, Health Maintenance Organizations, and other "coordinated care" plans offered by private insurers. These options will move Medicare, like the rest of the medical system, increasingly toward coordinated care, which sharply reduces the incentives for inflating costs that now exist. For those who choose one of the new options, the monthly Medicare premium (now $46 a month) would be replaced by a fee to the new provider that would usually be less than the current monthly deduction; for those who chose the fee-for-service system, they would pay more—as they should. Medicare would be preserved, saved from bankruptcy, and transformed into a system of consumer choice like the one Americans are themselves creating in the private sector.

By the standards of Washington, the People's Budget is a daring one. It is certain to bring howls of anguish from the vast establishment of the welfare state as well as others for whom federal bounty would cease. But we are confident that the People's Budget merits its title—that the vast majority of American citizens favor a dramatic downsizing of the government in Washington.

Our plan, taken in its entirety, will achieve a *truly* radical result—a shrinkage of the Washington government from the current 22 percent (and rising) of the nation's economy to less than 16 percent of the nation's economy, the lowest in nearly half a century. [See Figure 1.7] It would produce a dramatically less intrusive federal government by stopping federal bureaucrats from making detailed decisions about state, local, and even individual matters. It would balance the budget—and still permit much lower federal taxes than we presently have. Indeed, we would eliminate most federal sales taxes and cut the federal income tax by over 20 percent. That is the payoff,

Figure 1.7

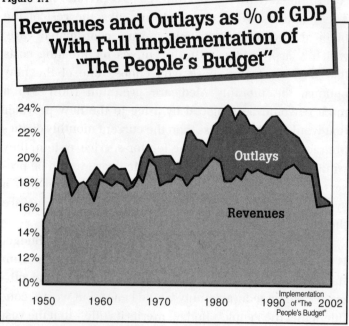

Revenues and Outlays as % of GDP With Full Implementation of "The People's Budget"

and it is worth fighting for.

Another payoff—one not discussed further in this book—involves Social Security. Social Security is a great, looming fiscal tidal wave threatening to devastate America's fiscal future. The facts are not in doubt: the so-called Social Security "trust fund" contains nothing more than IOUs from the federal government, and the IOUs will, by the time the baby boom reaches retirement age, add up to well over a trillion dollars. Dealing with the Social Security crisis is a challenge America will have to face before the decade is out. But we believe the budget crisis itself must be dealt with first and that doing so will create both the fiscal climate and the political momentum for tackling the Social Security problems.

Before turning to the proposals in the People's Budget, we offer in Chapter Two a brief history of the process by which America got into its current budget mess. ★

CHAPTER TWO

The Budget Mess

A Brief History

President Reagan used to tell his close advisors that the budget deficit was like a thermometer: the higher it went, the more heat the people in Congress would feel to reduce government. As in so many cases, Reagan had found a powerful metaphor, because the federal budget is much more than an accountants' report; it is an expression of everything the government does, a blueprint for American government. By the same token, the deficit is a measure of much more than a fiscal imbalance; it is a measure of how far out of step the government is with the people. When Americans refuse to pay for their government, they send a message: They want change.

Consider just how far out of balance we are. The annual deficit—the excess of expenditures over receipts—has been more than $149 billion for twelve consecutive years, and in eight of those years it was more than $200 billion. No end is in sight. The momentum of federal spend-

ing is such that if nothing is done, deficits in the $200 bil-
lion range will continue for a few more years (this is
President Clinton's proposal in
the 1996 budget)—and then the
deficit will again begin to
increase.

> **"I** would like to
> see the government
> run like a business.
> If you don't have the
> money, then you
> shouldn't spend it."

The national debt—which
is the cumulative result of all
the budget deficits (and surpluses) in the nation's history—
has risen to about *$3.5 trillion,*
[See Figure 2.1] and to nearly
$5 trillion if we include the debt the government owes to
its own trust funds, such as the Social Security Trust Fund.

Because of the large annual deficits, the debt held by
the public has grown faster than the nation's economic

Figure 2.1

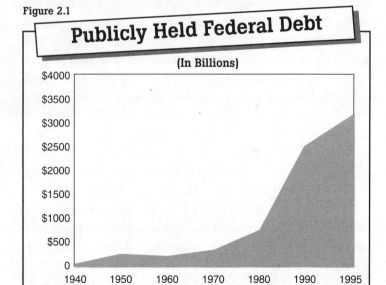

Publicly Held Federal Debt

(In Billions)

output, which is measured by the gross domestic product (GDP). The ratio of the government debt to the GDP provides a good measure of the nation's ability to make good on its borrowing. That ratio fell steadily after World War II, from 114 percent (meaning the debt was larger than the GDP) to only 25 percent in the mid-1970s, but, ominously, it has climbed back up to almost 52 percent today. The United States is not in nearly as bad a fix in this respect as some other countries, notably our northern neighbor Canada, but the situation is clearly worrisome. If nothing else, the big debt requires a large annual payment of interest, which in 1995 will be about $230 billion—or 15 percent of total federal spending—and by 1997 will actually exceed spending for national defense. This rising interest burden will be borne by our children and grandchildren—a situation that the Cato Institute has aptly termed "fiscal child abuse."

> **"Any kind of debt makes me nervous, but a debt of that size is just mindboggling. When will it stop?"**

Although the nation has run occasional sizable deficits in the past during war or deep economic depression, large annual deficits repeated year after year are a phenomenon only of the past twenty years. The Constitution did not require the federal government to balance its budget, but a rough balance between revenues and spending was the norm for most of our history. Deficit spending was frowned upon. The political system—the president and Congress—restrained itself. What went wrong?

Part of the explanation is the emergence of new economic theories, generally termed "Keynesian" after the
British economist John Maynard Keynes, which found that
deficits were beneficial under some circumstances. The
effects of this new excuse for deficit spending on the
American political system were far more damaging than
Keynes could ever have imagined. Once deficits attained a
certain respectability, the restraint on the politicians
diminished.

Another part of the explanation is a paradox—the
otherwise wholly desirable success of the Federal Reserve
in halting the rapid inflation of the late 1970s. The collapse
of inflation in the early 1980s had the incidental effect of
reducing the government's revenues way below what had
been anticipated when the budgets were drawn up.
Inflation, by swelling tax receipts, had disguised the serious underlying deficit situation. When inflation subsided,
the fallacy was exposed in the form of lower revenues and
bigger deficits than anyone had planned or foreseen.

Still another part of the problem, in the 1988–91 period, was the wholly unforeseen crisis in the savings and
loan industry, which led to huge outlays for deposit insurance. The deposit insurance system did its job, in that a
financial panic or crisis was averted. But at the peak of
deposit insurance outlays in 1991 the cost to the budget
was more than $65 billion. Incidentally, as the government
began to sell off the assets it had acquired from the insol-
vent banks and thrift institutions after 1992, the budget
received a temporary but large "bonus" that artificially
reduced the deficit, particularly in fiscal year 1993.

Democrats like to blame the emergence of large
deficits on President Reagan, whose program included tax

reduction and a badly needed increase in defense spending. It is true that the deficit, already sizable in the late 1970s, increased sharply in the Reagan period. But blaming the problem on Ronald Reagan is far too simplistic.

All the sophisticated arguments and explanations cannot disguise the underlying truth about the deficit problem and its fundamental cause: *The large deficits have come about not because revenues fell—they rose. Nor was defense spending the reason; the deficit has grown even as defense spending has fallen.* [See Figure 2.2]

The problem, in short, is the *size* of the federal government itself. The statistics speak for themselves. In the 1930s, even after the explosion of federal spending programs in the New Deal, total federal spending each year was 11 percent or less of the GDP. Spending rose massively, of course, in World War II. The nation came out of the

Figure 2.2

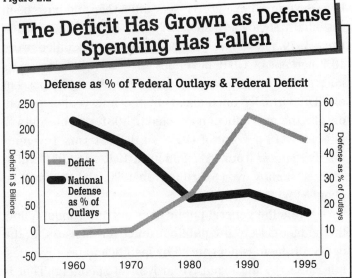

The Deficit Has Grown as Defense Spending Has Fallen

Defense as % of Federal Outlays & Federal Deficit

war with a larger defense establishment and also with a
permanently larger role for the federal government as
New Deal programs such as Social Security began to show
steady increases in spending. Still, in the 1950s federal
spending averaged only 18 percent of GDP, half of this on
defense as required by the Cold War.

As recently as 1965 total federal spending was only
about 17.5 percent of GDP. By 1983 it was over 24 percent
of GDP, and it has been at or above 22 percent for the last
fifteen years. This is so even though defense spending
began to *decline* as a share of GDP after 1986 (it did rise
slightly in 1991 because of the Gulf War). Meanwhile,
although there have been various tax reductions and tax
increases, revenues in most years for the past three
decades have been in the range of 18 to 19 percent of GDP
and higher in some years.

It is a myth that the deficit problem is a revenue problem. Revenues have grown year after year and have been
essentially steady as a share of GDP. Federal revenues in
fiscal 1979, just before President Reagan took office, were
19.1 percent of GDP. Revenues in fiscal 1989, ten years
later just as Reagan was leaving office, were 19.2 percent
of GDP, virtually unchanged. In the intervening period,
despite the tax reduction enacted in 1981, revenues never
fell below 18 percent of GDP. In dollar terms, revenues
nearly *doubled* from $517 billion in 1980 to $1,031 billion
(that is, slightly over $1 trillion) in 1990, and they will be
about $1.35 trillion in 1995.

While the general public does not and cannot follow
the budget closely, the public instinctively senses that the
deficit problem is not caused by insufficient tax revenues,
but rather by the explosive growth of spending. That is

why the resistance to higher taxes is so great, and that resistance is justified.

Federal spending has also grown far faster than inflation. If total federal outlays had grown no faster than the consumer price index in the past twenty years, the budget would have a massive surplus this year instead of a massive deficit of $200 billion!

A second truth is this: *Once the genie was out of the bottle and large deficits became the norm, the political system, and particularly the Congress, found it impossible to take the hard measures needed to curtail domestic spending and end the deficits.* Members of Congress bewailed the debt they were leaving to our children and grandchildren, but they were incapable of doing anything about it. And they admitted their paralysis. That is why support for a constitutional amendment to require a balanced budget consistently hovers around 75 percent.

> **"Trying to find further ways for money to come out of our pockets is ludicrous. I won't stand for another tax increase with all that waste around. We've got to look at where we're spending all that money."**

A principal reason for the paralysis of the political system in the face of large deficits lies in a third truth: *The federal budget is now dominated by "entitlements"—benefit programs in which eligible beneficiaries are automatically entitled to their payments without annual appropriations by Congress or any control by the president.* Entitlements are now about 50 percent of the budget.

Thirty years ago, in 1965, total mandatory program

spending (the term covering entitlements and a few other automatic, unappropriated spending programs) was $34 billion. By 1975—with the impact of President Johnson's Great Society initiatives such as Medicare, rising Social Security benefits and caseloads, and other factors—it had risen to $160 billion. Ten years later, in 1985, it was $433 billion. And in 1995 it is $792 billion! Mandatory spending in 1995 is *more than twenty-three times as great as it was thirty years earlier.*

It is only fair to note that inflation was a factor during this thirty-year period—at times serious, double-digit inflation. But even after adjusting for inflation, the rise in entitlement spending is staggering. The increase in constant 1987 dollars from 1965 to 1995 is from $115 billion to $594 billion, meaning that real spending on entitlements *quintupled* in thirty years.

Unlike "discretionary" programs, which can at least theoretically be curtailed through the annual appropriations process, the growth of entitlement spending can be curbed only by an affirmative act of Congress to change the underlying law that created the entitlement in the first place. Such changes might involve reducing benefits or making some beneficiaries ineligible. As any politician will affirm, it is far easier to deny *new* benefits or decline to create *new* programs than to take away benefits that already exist.

The explosion of entitlements has been fostered by a subtle, little noticed change in the way Congress handles government spending, a change that can be termed "balkanization" of spending control. For much of our history all government spending was in the hands of a single committee in each House of Congress—the Appropriations

Committees. They performed on the whole responsibly by trying to keep spending within the bounds set by the available revenues. But the big entitlement programs are created by other committees whose natural inclination is to respond to pressure from constituents to spend more, such as the Agricultural and Veterans Committees. The Appropriations Committees have no control over entitlements, which are enacted in separate legislation and create spending that, as we have noted, is automatic.

Entitlement spending is also bedeviled by the strange Washington practice of "baseline" budgeting. In brief, Congress takes credit for "cuts" in entitlement programs that are not cuts at all. As we shall see in a later chapter, Medicare is the champion example of this. Nearly every year it is "cut"—with accompanying large headlines and moans from the groups representing the elderly, hospitals, and doctors—and yet its spending increases by 9–10 percent year after year after year.

A baseline is a projection of what spending will be if Congress does nothing and leaves the present law alone. It can be a useful tool of budgeting. But in practice it has mischievous effects. For example, Congress can enact a provision on Medicare premiums that produces budget savings and lasts, by statute, for one year. The baseline assumes that this provision of law is allowed to expire on schedule. Then Congress extends the law for another year and claims "savings" of billions of dollars! And it does the same thing the next year! And each time, the press dutifully reports that Congress has passed a "cut" in Medicare.

Sometimes the claimed "savings" never happen at all. For example, the Omnibus Farm Bill of 1990 was widely advertised as cutting spending by about $11 billion

from the projections in force at that time. Instead, actual
spending in the five years (the final year's exact total is still
not known) will be over $55 billion, instead of the $41 billion estimated at the time of the 1990 "reforms." So what
was advertised as a $11 billion cut (from $52 billion to $41
billion) actually turned out to be a $3 billion increase.

In any case, real cuts in entitlements are undoubtedly difficult politically. The biggest of them—Social Security
and Medicare—benefit mainly the elderly and have nearly
40 million beneficiaries. Some entitlements, mostly for
people with low or no incomes, are in the "welfare" category and will be discussed in a later chapter. But other
large programs—such as the federal civilian and military
retirement programs—benefit people who are not poor
but understandably feel they deserve these benefits.

The paralysis created by a budget dominated by entitlements can be put another way. *Congress can avoid cutting entitlements, or reject presidential proposals to cut
them, simply by doing nothing.* And that is precisely what
Congress did in the Reagan and Bush years to presidential
proposals to reform entitlements. Furthermore, the presidential veto power has no impact in the area of entitlements because there are no bills to veto. Appropriations,
"discretionary" spending, have to be acted on every year.
But entitlement spending, like the Energizer Bunny, just
keeps "going and going and going."

Unfortunately, the fourth truth is that Congress'
inability to control spending is not limited to entitlements:
*Despite a prevailing mythology to the contrary, domestic
discretionary spending—the part appropriated each year
and presumably controllable—has not been curtailed in the
last ten years.* This is the spending Congress loves best. It

contains the "pork barrel" projects that gratify constituents, from teachers to subway riders.

Despite a supposed squeeze on domestic discretionary spending in the Reagan budgets and a new system of "caps" on this spending that started in 1990, it too has exploded. Indeed, this category of the budget rose from $146 billion in fiscal year 1985 to $260 billion in fiscal 1995, an increase of 78 percent—nearly as large a percentage increase as that for entitlement or mandatory spending in the same ten-year period.

In the five-year period since the caps—1990 to 1995—the growth of domestic discretionary spending has been $77 billion, or 42 percent. Even measured in constant dollars—that is, adjusting for inflation—domestic discretionary spending rose 25 percent from 1985 to 1995 and 20 percent from 1990 to 1995, the period of the caps.

There are various reasons why the caps have not, in fact, had the hoped-for effect. Some are quite technical, and we need not go into them here. Suffice it to say that the seemingly tight restraints—which Congress moans about year after year and the press accepts as real—are revealed, long after nobody is looking, to have been not so tight after all. Congress has been pretending that it has been living on a diet—and many of the members even believe that it has—when in fact it has been eating quite heartily.

We have told the story of how the deficit mess came about. To recap: The problem arose partly from some unforeseen factors, such as the collapse of inflation and the savings and loan crisis. But the underlying cause was really very simple—the unrestrained growth of spending by the government in Washington. ★

CHAPTER THREE

Ending the Myth of Federal Compassion

The era of centralized bureaucratic power that began with the New Deal, unsurprisingly, brought with it an ethic of centralized, bureaucratic compassion. As Dr. Marvin Olasky discusses in his path-breaking book, *The Tragedy of American Compassion*[1], the New Deal—and to a much greater extent, the Great Society bureaucratic welfare programs—replaced a community-based, personal, and far more effective system of helping those in need.

At the time, it must have seemed the right thing to do. Big was better, and a "scientific," centrally controlled approach to helping the poor no doubt made sense in a world in which big institutions were succeeding at everything else. In addition, some would argue, income inequalities and cultural differences between states called for direct involvement by the federal government.

---

[1] Marvin Olasky, *The Tragedy of American Compassion* (Washington, D.C.: Regnery, 1992).

But in the last thirty years, we have learned that institutional compassion—and certainly *federal* compassion—is a destructive myth. It is time to turn welfare back to the people, to their communities, and to the states. That is what this chapter proposes.

> **"W**e're losing the American Dream, because we're losing the American family. It all goes back to the family, and welfare destroys the family."

"Welfare" means different things to different people. To some people, it means only the familiar, sixty-year-old program of Aid to Families With Dependent Children (AFDC). Others think "welfare" is any and every program of government assistance for individuals, except perhaps Social Security.

To most people, and to the authors, "welfare" means government programs that give cash and in-kind benefits only to people who can show they are poor—that is, benefit programs that are means-tested. These programs are mostly entitlements—AFDC, Food Stamps, Supplemental Security Income (SSI—cash assistance for the needy elderly, blind, and disabled), Medicaid, child nutrition (mostly subsidized school lunches), and a few smaller programs. Entitlements, as we noted in Chapter Two, are open-ended: everyone who qualifies under the terms of the program gets the benefits, and there is no annual control by Congress over the amount spent.

Other welfare programs are "discretionary," i.e., they are limited by the available funds and not everyone eligible receives the benefit. This category includes subsidized housing of various kinds, the WIC program (food supplements for needy Women, Infants, and Children), low-income energy assistance, and several other small programs.

The total cost to the federal government of all these programs, entitlement and discretionary, in fiscal year 1995 is over $200 billion. By far the costliest program is Medicaid at $88 billion. The other large items are food stamps ($27 billion), SSI ($24 billion), subsidized housing ($24.5 billion), and AFDC and related "family support" payments ($17 billion). Medicaid and AFDC are federal–state programs, with the states doing the administering, guided by various federal mandates, and the federal government paying the majority of the cost. [See Figure 3.1]

While the poor, of course, have always been with us,

Figure 3.1

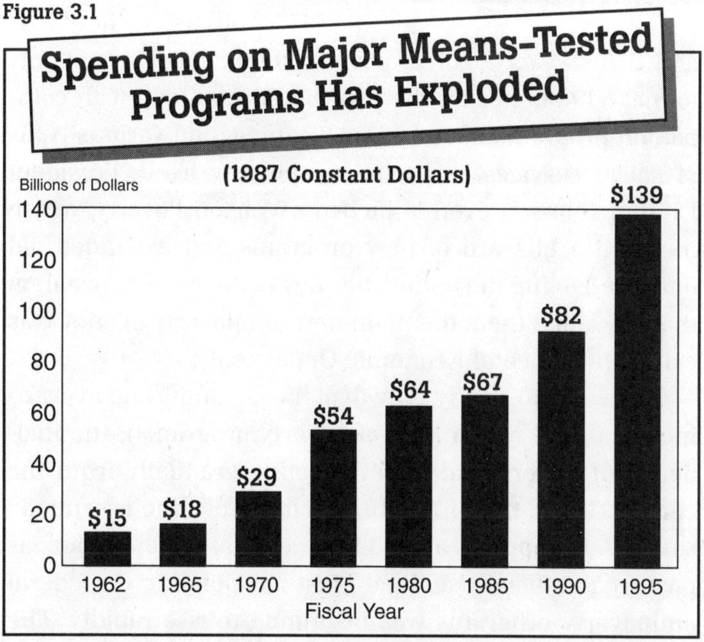

Spending on Major Means-Tested Programs Has Exploded

Billions of Dollars   **(1987 Constant Dollars)**

Fiscal Year	Amount
1962	$15
1965	$18
1970	$29
1975	$54
1980	$64
1985	$67
1990	$82
1995	$139

for most of American history they were not considered a federal responsibility. Indeed, none of the programs discussed here even existed at the federal level until at least the 1930s. Instead, state and local relief programs, and countless private charities, provided help for the poor. As Olasky documents in *The Tragedy of American Compassion*, this locally based system provided much more personal and, arguably, more effective help than today's large welfare bureaucracy.

"The problem with a lot of these welfare programs is that they start off with good intentions, but then they can't be derailed."

Every one of the programs listed above—some starting in the 1930s, others in the 1960s and 1970s—was begun as a well-intentioned effort not only to make life better for the poor but also—along with companion programs in education, training, and various types of social services—to help end poverty itself. President Lyndon Johnson even launched a War on Poverty, which included a blizzard of new programs and expanded old ones. Reflecting the optimistic view of the poverty problem that prevailed then, the main new antipoverty agency was called the Office of Economic Opportunity.

Thanks to steady growth of the economy and average incomes (and not to federal poverty programs), the incidence of poverty did in fact decline gradually from the early 1940s to the 1970s. But then the decline essentially stopped. It stopped—at 13–14 percent of the population, as poverty is officially defined—just as spending on federal antipoverty programs was beginning to rise rapidly. The

United States saw a sustained, if not spectacular, growth of the economy in the 1980s, and the creation of more than two million jobs a year—but the poverty rate barely budged.

At about the same time the War on Poverty was getting under way, there was a dramatic increase in births out of wedlock (presently two-thirds of black births and over 20 percent among whites). Many of the births are to teenagers, and a large proportion of the unmarried mothers, teenage and older, are on welfare. The result has been generations of children who grow up without fathers, a phenomenon most social scientists believe, and common sense suggests, has led in turn to many of the problems of today's inner cities—crime, youth gangs, drugs, high dropout rates in school, and the creation of an intergenerational culture of poverty. Ultimately, the result has been the tragedy we all watch each night on television: the agony of young children growing up in conditions of poverty and violence we can hardly believe exist in America. [See Figure 3.2]

The public is correct in perceiving that the government poverty programs subsidize antisocial behavior, even if they do not literally cause it. The images of the "projects"—desolate public housing complexes, with urine on the walls and broken windows—are not fantasies. And the statistics on out-of-wedlock births and directly related crime rates are not fantasies. While our current welfare programs have provided a safety net for literally millions of people temporarily in need, they have also helped create the tragedy of the underclass. In this sense, the War on Poverty has been a terrible failure.

Welfare reform to date—mostly work requirements—

Figure 3.2

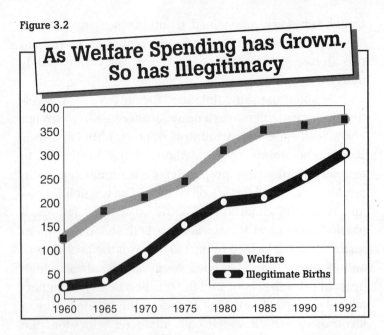

As Welfare Spending has Grown, So has Illegitimacy

has been limited and ineffective. Work requirements, unfortunately, have limited promise. How do you find a decently paying job for a young mother who can barely read and who is totally without useful skills and discipline? Telling her to "get a job" is neither realistic nor compassionate. Indeed, the numerous evaluation studies of welfare-to-work experiments in various states have shown very modest results in moving long-term welfare recipients off the rolls—even those who are capable of work.

Fraud is another element of the present system that is no fantasy of the heartless. Food stamps, as congressional testimony in early 1995 made clear and as many people already knew, are sometimes misused by recipients, even traded for drugs and alcohol. And it is not just recipients who take advantage of the system. Fraud by unscrupulous doctors and hospitals in the Medicaid program, for example, is well documented. The director of Florida's Medicaid Fraud Control Unit, Mark Schlein, said in early 1995 that "[t]he way Medicaid is set up, it provides an invitation to steal."

The recent explosion in the cost of SSI is an example of a welfare program going terribly wrong—though in this case with little public notice. Recently the *Baltimore Sun* reported (the story was picked up by *Reader's Digest*) on a woman in Louisiana who has managed by persistent effort and numerous appeals to get herself, her common-law husband, and her seven children all on SSI for "disability," meaning that the family gets nine checks from the government totaling $3,893 *every month.*

> **"You** can't just assume that people are going to play right. But sometimes we set up the system to encourage them to play wrong. Look at welfare."

SSI began as a federal program, replacing state programs in the early 1970s, mainly as an income supplement for the elderly, including those whose Social Security benefits were too low to support them. As Social Security benefit levels have increased, the number of low-income elderly—and hence the number of SSI recipients—has actually declined (though recently elderly *immigrants* have begun to swell the rolls again). So far, so good.

SSI also provides benefits for the disabled—clearly something else most Americans favor. But in recent years, the number of disabled SSI beneficiaries has skyrocketed, resulting in the doubling of SSI spending (after adjusting for inflation) since 1980. Has America suddenly been afflicted with a plague of disability? Or is something else going on?

As it turns out, many of the new SSI beneficiaries are not disabled in any ordinary sense—a physical disability that keeps them from being able to work. They are classified as "disabled" for mental reasons—or even for "social" ailments such as a chaotic upbringing or lack of a work ethic. One-fifth of the recipients are now *children*, who are eligible if they are unable to engage in "age-appropriate activities of daily living." Because SSI benefits are substantially larger than those of AFDC, it is sad but true that parents can and do, hold children out of school so that they fall behind, in order to meet the "age-appropriate" test. These parents are, in effect, collecting benefits for having created "disabilities" in their own children. SSI, begun with the best of all possible intentions, has become a perfect example of the welfare state gone wild.

Perhaps the most troubling consequence of this kind of abuse is what journalists have labeled "compassion fatigue"—a drop-off in people's willingness to support programs to help the poor. Polls conducted for the Times-Mirror Corporation show that the proportion of people who feel that government "has a responsibility to take care of people who can't take care of themselves" peaked at 74 percent in 1988, but has now fallen today to just 57 percent. And although private charitable programs are still a major component of the public assistance picture—nearly a quarter of all of it comes from charities—donations have dropped off in recent years.

The American people are compassionate, but there is a limit to their willingness to support a system that is riddled with abuse and helps to create a permanent underclass.

So what to do? Granting that welfare has failed, is real reform even possible? We are dealing, after all, with human behavior, and government is not very good at altering behavior for the better.

As 1995 began, with the new majority in Congress grimly determined to make some real changes, the air was filled with debate on the subject of welfare reform. Never have so many welfare mothers been seen on the TV screen in the family living room, as legislation moves through Congress. But as the debate made clear, solutions to the problem are anything but obvious.

James Q. Wilson, a scholar whose work is praised by people at both ends of the political spectrum, made this point in a recent (December 24, 1994) highly acclaimed article in the *Wall Street Journal,* "A New Approach to Welfare Reform: Humility." Noting a virtual "consensus" that the social plague of crime, drug abuse, teenage pregnancy, and welfare dependency results from a weakening of the family, Wilson wrote:

> [W]e must now face the fact that we don't know what to do about the problem. The American people are well ahead of their leaders in this regard. They doubt very much that government can do much of anything at all. They are not optimistic that any other institution can do much better, and they are skeptical that there will be a spontaneous regeneration of decency, commitment and personal responsibility.

According to Wilson, three main explanations are offered for the growth of the underclass and its associated pathologies. One group thinks the problem arises mainly from the loss of well-paying manufacturing and other jobs in the inner cities. Another argues with equal conviction that welfare itself is the cause of the problem, having become "sufficiently generous as to make the formation of stable two-parent families either irrational or unnecessary." A third school sees the problem as "cultural"—a condition in which "child rearing and family life as traditionally understood can no longer compete with or bring under prudent control a culture of radical self-indulgence and oppositional defiance, fostered by drugs, television, video games, street gangs, and predatory sexuality."

> **"The answer is definitely not more Washington. There are too many people running the show. Something else—anything else—must be better."**

All three versions of the problem are somewhat plausible. In the first, the solution presumably is jobs, through such devices as "enterprise zones" to attract businesses to the inner city. In the second, the solution is a radical reform of welfare, such as a rigid insistence on work in exchange for welfare and the end of incentives for single parenthood. In the third, the way out is to "alter the inner-city ethos by means of private redemptive movements supported by a system of shelters or group homes in which at-risk children and their young mothers can be given familial care and adult supervision in safe and drug-free settings."

The legislative "solutions" being pursued in Congress reflect one or another of these views—including rigid work requirements (the House Democratic bill) and the end of benefits for teenage mothers or for additional children (the leading Republican bill).

Wilson is skeptical. He has serious doubts about the efficacy of the solutions that spring from each of the three statements of the underlying cause of the welfare problem—the jobs solution, the radical welfare solution, or the "private redemptive movements" solution. For example, as he points out in discussing the reform-welfare solution, there are "important puzzles in the connection between welfare and child-bearing."

Wilson cites "great differences in illegitimacy rates across ethnic groups facing similar circumstances. . . . Clearly, there is some important cultural or at least noneconomic factor at work, one that has deep historical roots and that may vary with the size of the community and the character of the surrounding culture."

Ultimately, Wilson agrees with the vast majority of the people that, as starters, welfare ought to be turned back to individuals, private charities, communities, and states:

> [T]he federal government cannot have a meaningful family policy for the nation, and it ought not to try. Not only does it not know and cannot learn from experts what to do, but whatever it thinks it ought to do, it will try to do in the worst possible way. Which is to say, uniformly, systematically, politically and ignorantly. . . .[W]e ought to turn the task and the money for rebuilding lives, welfare payments, housing subsidies, the whole lot, over to cities and states and private agencies. . . .

That is what the People's Budget proposes to do.

Once it is accepted that the best hope of finding a solution for the welfare problem is to shift all the welfare programs to the states and localities, the question arises,

how exactly do we go about doing it? There are essentially two ways, one more radical—and more promising—
than the other.

The first and most familiar way comes under the
heading of "block grant." This is the route being suggested by congressional Republicans and supported by
Republican governors as the welfare debate develops and
intensifies.

Under the block grant approach, the federal government drops most or all strings, requirements, and prescrip-
tions for a program or group of programs, but continues its
financial support. A block grant covering several programs
is made to the states—distributed among them by an appropriate formula—to help them finance whatever the activity
may be. The states, not the federal government, set most or
all of the rules. They would be rid of nearly all federal
paperwork, at a considerable savings to them.

As a hypothetical example, if the federal cost of all
welfare benefit programs was $200 billion in 1995,
Congress would repeal all the thousands of pages of existing federal law and instead pass a simple law establishing
a new block grant to the states of, say $180 billion (the sav-
ings would reflect, among other things, a reduction in the
federal bureaucracy that has been supervising all these
programs). The grant would also be "capped" at some
fixed amount for each year in the future, perhaps with a
formula increasing the grant for inflation or some other
factor but not increasing it automatically if caseloads were
to rise. This approach could involve several block grants
(say one for cash assistance, one for nutrition, one for
housing).

Note that the simple act of capping the block grant

automatically ends the entitlement status of AFDC, food stamps, SSI, Medicaid, and so on, at least as far as the federal government is concerned. If the welfare or food stamp rolls were to grow under the new rules established by the states or if Medicaid costs were to continue to rise rapidly as they have been doing, there would be no increase in the financial obligation of the federal government—and thus no "unavoidable" increase in the budget deficit and the national debt because of "forces beyond our control."

The states could keep some or all of these programs as entitlements, if they wish. (Most already have "general assistance" entitlement programs that apply to needy adults who are not covered by the federal programs.) Or they could allot a fixed amount of money for each program based on estimates of the caseload; if the estimates were wrong and the caseload grew faster than expected, they could either impose a uniform reduction of benefits or adopt a "first-come, first-served" policy. This is precisely the kind of issue that should be—and would be—debated within each state.

In any case, under the block grant approach each state would essentially know in advance how much money it would get from Washington. It would then design its programs with this knowledge in mind. Unless the poverty problem greatly worsened, which does not seem likely, the financial strain on the states would be limited because of the large yearly lump sum of money from Washington. Regardless of the level of welfare benefits they chose to provide, virtually all states would gain from being able to design programs to meet their own specific needs.

The block grant approach has much to recommend it. As will be explained below, we propose it as a transition device in the more fundamental and radical solution to welfare. But as good as block grants are, they have two serious flaws.

The first is so obvious that it is often overlooked. It is inherently rather silly for the federal government to raise (in this case) $180 billion from federal taxpayers and then send the money right back to the states with no program rules and no control over how the money is spent. Why should the federal government raise the money in the first place?

If the states are to have control over the panoply of welfare programs, then logically the state taxpayers—not the federal taxpayers—should pay for them. Federal taxes should be reduced, and states should raise taxes as much as they feel is required to get the job done. The argument is not whether federal taxes are "better" or "worse" than state taxes, but rather whether the level of government that runs a program should raise the taxes to pay for it.

The second flaw in block grants is a corollary of the first. If money comes "free" from Washington, the normal human inclination is to be less careful in spending it. And there are plenty of examples. Democrats, who typically prefer to retain federal strings on federal programs, pointed out a few of these in opposing an early 1995 Republican block grant proposal to replace existing federal crime programs. During debate in the House Judiciary Committee, the Democrats cited abuses that had arisen under a previous crime control block grant operated by a federal agency called the Law Enforcement Assistance Administration. To quote the *New York Times* account of the debate in the committee:

> Detailing some of the abuses under the agency,

Democrats said that a local sheriff in Louisiana had bought a tank; that Indiana had bought an aircraft that was meant for police use but instead transported the governor and his family on personal trips, including one to pick up a moon rock, and that Philadelphia had spent $265,000 for a report on a project on treatment of drug addiction that produced a report with only one paragraph on the effect of the project.

In addition, states often try to "game" the system, sweeping as much activity as they can under the federal grant umbrella in order to get more federal dollars. To cite one state budget official who speaks for many of his colleagues, "We have always done a good job of maxing out on federal dollars."

The result is a predictable cycle. Block grants are enacted. States spend the money on senseless things, or "game" the system to get more money. Congress responds by tightening the federal strings. And

> **"When** the government—or anyone—is forced to spend their money or lose it, it encourages waste."

eventually, what started out as a "no-strings-attached" block grant becomes just another micro-managed-from-Washington welfare program.

Although even with these potential abuses, block grants are arguably better than prescriptive federal laws, experience shows they do not work over the long run. And the idea of raising funds from federal taxpayers, only to send them back to the states with "no strings attached" is inherently illogical. So if federal responsibility for welfare is to be replaced by state responsibility, as the American people so clearly want, it should be done completely—

including lowering the level of federal taxation.

A total transfer of all welfare programs and functions to the states must, of course, be done carefully. (Housing programs, for reasons outlined below, are a special case and must remain federal, although transformed and greatly improved, for some years to come.) The transfer of welfare to the states should follow three principles:

★ The final termination of the federal role must be set a few years from now to give the states time to adjust, *but it must be known and fixed by law now,* to provide as much certainty as is possible in a democratic system.
★ Transition assistance in the form of federal block grants should be given in the intervening period.
★ The end of federal responsibility for all welfare programs *must be accompanied by a firm commitment to reduce federal taxes at a given date in the future,* coinciding with the date the states assume complete responsibility for welfare.

Our proposal is simple: Legislation should be passed this year establishing a date—we suggest the year 2000—when states will take over complete responsibility for most federal welfare programs, including Medicaid. The legislation would also specify the federal tax cuts that would take place at the same time, so that the reduction of federal welfare spending would be matched very closely by the reduction in both federal excise taxes and individual income taxes. As discussed in detail in Chapter Eight, the total of "tax resources" made available to the states will approximately offset the loss of federal dollars.

But this will not be so for each state. The federal tax

reduction, as it reduces tax collections in a given state, may be more or less than the federal dollars spent on the welfare-related programs in that state. There will be some winners and some losers.

We propose to compensate the losers, mostly the relatively poorer states—that is, those with lower-than-average per capita income. The compensation plan we have adopted involves federal lump-sum grants totaling about $26 billion in the year 2000 to about half the states. The outlay for the compensation grants is included in our budget totals.

While the compensation total of about $26 billion is small relative to the total amount of federal spending being cut, almost all of the states that currently receive significantly more in federal spending than they pay in federal taxes are relatively small in population, such as Arkansas, Kentucky, Louisiana, Maine, Mississippi, Montana, New Mexico, South Dakota, Rhode Island, Vermont, and West Virginia. Because they are small these states can be compensated fully with the relatively small total amount we propose.[2]

To avoid the need for further votes by Congress—that is, opportunities for backsliding—the initial legislation would contain a formula for determining the size of the tax cut five years hence. It would specify a minimum tax cut to accompany the welfare transfer that would take place in any event. But beyond the minimum tax cut, it would leave the exact size of the reduction to be determined later by the formula, in light of events.

---

[2] New York is the major exception, primarily because its Medicaid program under former Governor Cuomo was the most expensive and wasteful in the country, but major reforms are under way under its new leadership.

Between now and 2000, states would receive interim block grants from the federal government, with enough flexibility to set their own rules. The block grants would be designed so as to avoid "gaming" by the states; for example, states could not get more money by just letting their welfare programs grow and states that had done a good job of controlling costs or reducing poverty would not be punished.

To the extent federal rules and mandates continue to exist for some programs during the transition, a liberal "waiver" authority is crucial. Some states, for example, are ready to make major changes in Medicaid but cannot under the current prescriptive federal law. The legislation proposed here would grant waivers almost automatically to states that want to change the system, including changes in the eligible population and how they receive medical services.

The end of federal mandates in some programs such as Medicaid would itself curb growth. In the first stage of the transition, in 1996–97, there would be separate block grants for cash assistance, nutrition, and medical care. During this stage, the federal government could still seek to curb the growth of welfare programs or direct them to some extent, perhaps through some of the benefit limitation proposals currently being considered in Congress.

In the second phase, in 1998–99, preparing the way for complete state takeover, there would be a single large block grant to each state to cover most, but not all, of the federal cost of the whole package of welfare programs in that state. Any remaining federal rules would wither away.

All of these provisions would be part of the initial 1995 legislation. The states would know just where they stood. And then the states, knowing that a federal tax cut was in the cards, could decide how to run the programs—eligibility, benefit levels, cash or food stamps, duration of benefits, and so on—and could begin to decide whether and how much to raise taxes to make up for the loss of federal dollars starting in the year 2000. These would be lively major issues in state elections in 1996, 1997, and 1998.

American taxpayers—taken collectively—would of course receive a net tax cut. Federal bureaucracy would shrink. States would experiment with new, more effective ways of dealing with poverty. And, because states cannot finance runaway welfare spending through deficits as the federal government can, they would have a far more powerful incentive to reduce the number of people in poverty and so control costs. Indeed, some states have already shown a greater ability to restrain welfare spending and cut welfare rolls than the federal government—without denying aid to the truly needy.

Although all sorts of dire predictions will be made by defenders of the government in Washington, there is absolutely no reason—in 1995—to assume that states are less compassionate than are bureaucrats in Washington, D.C. Changing the welfare system we now have is not the same thing as denying a safety net to the needy. Senator Bob Packwood put it well: "Why should we assume that state officials will be any less sensitive than we are to the problems of children and the disabled? Why presume that they will be evil or malicious?" The states will approach the problems of poverty differently, and some will be more "liberal" than others. But there is a wealth of evidence that the American people want to help the poor and good reason to believe they will help more if they feel their money is being sensibly spent to help people close to home.

The cry will go up—has already gone up—"What of the children?" Here again, we agree with James Q. Wilson in his article cited above when he said that "our overriding goal ought to be to save the children." It is precisely because the current welfare system is condemning so many children to lives of poverty and abuse that we—and the American people—insist on dramatic reform.

We must not forget that to continue to do what we are doing also has consequences for our children. An anonymous respondent to a recent public opinion survey spoke for millions when he said, "What is the most important reason to eliminate the federal deficit and balance the budget? For the future American generations, for the children." What troubles Americans most about deficits and debt is the legacy they leave to the children, including the mounting interest payments.

> **"We've tried to make everything so easy for our kids. We've created programs for every situation. Now look at what we've done. They think they deserve everything."**

This worry is real. *All* children, no matter what their income background, have a stake in getting the federal budget under control. When there is loud lamenting of the presumed bad consequences for poor children of this or that major reform, those who lament are ignoring the benefits to the vast majority of children who will pay if the federal spending spree is not curtailed.

Moreover, the states will hardly allow poor children to starve. Some may find the road toward a better psychological and emotional future for the neglected and often abused offspring of the poor. After all, all of us are seeking reform precisely *because* of what is happening to the children in the present system.

Alice Rivlin, President Clinton's budget director, made an important point in this connection in her recent book, *Reviving the American Dream,* published shortly before she joined the administration. Although Ms. Rivlin does not advocate terminating the federal role in welfare entitlements, she does propose an almost equally radical shift of federal domestic programs and activities to the states. Citing the worry "often expressed by traditional liberals" that states "will neglect the less fortunate," Ms. Rivlin says:

> The fear has some basis, but poor and minority young people will not be left out if states play an aggressive role in economic development. Improving education, skills and opportunities for the future labor force necessarily involves concentrating on the futures of low-income and minority young people, because they will make up such a large part of that labor force. Indeed, effective action to improve the skills and job prospects of the poor, especially young people, seems more likely if it is seen as essential to community and state economic development than if it is seen as federally funded redistribution policy.

But what if the states do not fully pick up the slack? What, in the worst case, if some mothers now on welfare ultimately find themselves with no source of funds for themselves and their children? Congressman Jim McCrery has a tough but reasoned response to this concern:

> If a single woman with a couple of kids just can't find or keep a job, or get help from family or neighbors, she will have an option to give her children up for adoption, place them in a group setting or foster care. Will some people have a hard time? Yes. Is that price worth it for the good of generations to come? Yes.

Many Americans nevertheless want to maintain some federal role in helping the needy, especially helping those who help themselves by working and behaving responsibly. The hard part is finding a way to do that without creating incentives for the very behavior we want to discourage.

"Washington is incredibly inefficient. It's like a bad charity that spends more on administration than on the people it's supposed to benefit."

We offer three specific proposals for things the federal government can and, at least for the foreseeable future, ought to do or start doing. We propose:

★ **First,** a brand-new, very substantial tax credit for charitable donations to organizations that help the poor
★ **Second,** to reform the Earned Income Tax Credit (EITC) to supplement the income of low-income working people with children and encourage them to advance into better jobs
★ **Third,** to radically transform housing assistance for poor families, converting it from a system of subsidies

that go to local government housing agencies and landlords to a system of vouchers that go directly to those in need.

TAX CREDITS FOR CHARITABLE CONTRIBUTIONS

Consider three questions:

★ **First,** should the federal government guarantee everyone a minimum income, even if they are able-bodied and choose not to work? The people's answer to that question is clearly *no.*

★ **Second,** does every successful American have an obligation—in some way of their own choosing—to help provide for those in need? We believe the answer to that question, for most people, is yes.

★ **Third,** given that successful Americans should help those in need, does it follow that the only way to do that is to require them to send tax dollars to Washington to be spent by large, centralized bureaucracies? The answer to this question is clearly no.

From the beginning of this nation—and long before federal welfare programs—private charitable organizations have offered help of many kinds to the poor, from soup kitchens to care of the sick. Currently, private charities provide nearly $200 billion a year, in cash or in kind, for health, education, and welfare. (This does not include nonprofit organizations in such areas as medical research or the local opera company.) In 1991 more than $100 billion was provided in cash for welfare-type charities, given

by the 72 percent of American households that made contributions. And Americans volunteered over 15 billion
hours of their time, the equivalent of nine million full-time
employees, to organized charities.

Most Americans feel that private charities do better at
taking care of those in need
than the federal government
does. In one recent poll, 52 percent said that charities are
"much better" at taking care of
people who can't take care of
themselves, compared with
only 34 percent who said "we
need the government in
Washington" to do it.

"I have confidence in the American Dream because I have confidence in Americans to do the right thing."

Yet most Americans receive no incentives to contribute to charities, because charitable contributions are
deductible against the federal income tax only for the
roughly 25 percent of taxpayers who itemize deductions—
i.e., those with the highest incomes.

Thus we propose a dollar for dollar tax credit, up to
$500, for contributions made to charities that help the
poor. And we propose that the credit should be available to
all, whether or not they itemize deductions.

The practical implication of this proposal is simply
this: If you want to, you can pay your $500 to the govern-
ment in Washington. To the extent taxpayers do not claim
the credit, the money will go into a new compensation
block grant fund and be distributed to the states along with
the equalization funds described above.

Or you might choose to give $500 to a local charity
that runs a soup kitchen or takes care of unwed mothers.

If so, you could take $500 off your taxes.

In effect, a family would choose whether to give up to $500 to Uncle Sam or to the Salvation Army. Which do you think it would choose?

The Internal Revenue Service (IRS) would certify charities eligible for the new credit. The rest of the charities would continue to be eligible for the present charitable deduction, as would contributions over and above $500 to the designated public assistance charities.

This proposal would ensure that the first $500 every family now pays in taxes—about $40 billion altogether—would go to support public assistance programs, either through the federal government or through the charity of their choice.

A tax credit of this kind would enable private organizations, with all their ability to experiment and innovate, to assume a larger share of the burden of dealing with the problems of the poor, including poor children. As noted in the preceding section, we know that government programs have failed. And we know that there is no better source of innovative and truly compassionate approaches to poverty than the myriad institutions and individuals that make up the nation's private charities.

A NEW AND IMPROVED EARNED INCOME TAX CREDIT

The EITC provides an income supplement for the "working poor." For almost every recipient, the EITC is larger than what he or she owes in taxes; because the credit is "refundable," they actually receive a cash payment from the federal government. Indeed, over 80 percent of the cost of the EITC is in cash payments.[3]

The EITC, about twenty years old, is the newest of the large entitlement programs. Partly because more and more of the eligible population is collecting the benefits, but mainly because of successive liberalizations of the benefit structure, the EITC is now the fastest growing of the entitlement programs, growing faster even than Medicare. Spending is projected to rise from $9 billion in 1993 to $25 billion in 2000—nearly *tripling* in seven years.

Although the EITC is a good idea in principle—providing an incentive for poor Americans to work, while supplementing their incomes—in practice it mostly discourages work. At incomes above about $11,600 the program imposes a serious disincentive to earn more, because it effectively levies a high "tax" in the form of reduced benefits. The more you make from your job, the less you get from the EITC, which means that if you get a $1,000 raise, your take home pay goes up by $1,000 minus the cut in your EITC—just like a tax.

The disincentive to work imposed by the EITC is very significant. In fact, EITC recipients who make between roughly $16,000 and $28,500 a year pay a total marginal tax rate of over 43 percent—about the same as people making high six-figure incomes!

A second problem with the EITC is that it encourages people to overreport their income. Since—at low incomes—earning more money gets you a higher EITC payment, you can increase your check from the government by reporting more earnings to the IRS than you actu-

[3] The Clinton administration was very misleading in 1993 when, in describing its overall budget package, it listed a liberalization of the EITC as a "tax cut," to be offset against the major tax increases in the program, rather than a spending increase, which is what it was.

ally make. Because the IRS has no mechanism for stopping this sort of tax cheating (it worries more about underreporting!), there are no solid estimates on the extent of the problem—but many experts believe it is substantial.

It *is* possible, however, to accomplish the EITC's two main purposes—to offset the Social Security tax for those with low incomes and to encourage work at the very low end of the income scale—while limiting the disincentives to work and discouraging cheating.

The new EITC we propose would consist of two new tax credits. Like the current EITC, these would be *refundable*—that is, people who owe little or no tax would get a check from the IRS. Also, like the current EITC, they would be available only to parents with children. Because of their technical nature, we describe the details of these new credits in Appendix Two. Their effects, however, are worth summarizing here:

★ The "working poor"—those at the lowest end of the income spectrum—would receive larger subsidies and hence larger incentives to work.

★ The benefits would be based only on the first $10,000 of income, so that the incentive to cheat by overreporting income would be reduced.

★ The disincentives to work would be dramatically reduced. Under the current EITC, ten families are discouraged from working for every one that is encouraged; under this proposal, the ratio would fall from 10:1 to 1.5:1. The top effective marginal tax rate on people in the $16,000–$28,500 income range would be cut nearly in half, from 43 percent to roughly 22 percent.

This reform would stop the explosion of spending on

the EITC that would otherwise occur. But its more important effect would be to strengthen the incentive to work for the poorest people.

HOUSING PROGRAMS

Public housing, as we all know, is one of the horror stories of the welfare state. The "projects" has become a familiar term among people across the income spectrum, and one recent documentary referred to the federal Department of Housing and Urban Development (HUD) as "America's slumlord." The People's Budget proposes to get the federal government out of the housing business. (Note: The problems of the cities are very real. While the federal government cannot solve them all, it has created some of them, and an aggressive effort to examine and reform federal policies that affect the cities—from environmental policy to the criminal justice system—is certainly warranted. But this is a separate issue from preserving HUD and/or current programs.)

Ending the entire federal role in housing is not simple. The long-term contracts that exist cannot just be canceled. It is, however, possible to make a simple, yet radical change: *All housing assistance to poor people would be converted to rental vouchers. The subsidy would go to people, not to buildings.*

We discuss the details and rationale of this proposal in Appendix Two. Here we would make only three points:

★ **First,** changing our policies toward public housing is a moral imperative. For the federal government to be housing mothers and children in projects riddled with drugs and crime is wrong—especially when commission after commission, over more than thirty years, has recommended dramatic change.

★ **Second,** the proposals we offer are similar in principle to what HUD Secretary Henry Cisneros has offered, which in turn are similar to those offered by former Secretary Jack Kemp. Moving from "project-based" to "tenant-based" assistance is a common-sense change that has widespread support.

★ **Third,** federal spending on housing is a large and growing part of the federal budget—approaching $25 billion in 1995. By moving to a system of tenant-based assistance that is not only more compassionate but also more efficient, we can significantly reduce federal spending. Indeed, when fully implemented, the proposals described in detail in Appendix Two would reduce federal spending by as much as $3 billion annually. (Note: Because of prior commitments, however, outlays would continue to grow for the next several years.)

CONCLUSION

The thirty-year experiment with massive federal welfare programs has failed. It has created disincentives to work, discouraged family formation, built slums, and contributed to the creation of a self-sustaining "underclass" that is increasingly alienated from mainstream American culture. By sapping resources from states, communities, and individuals, it has discouraged the kinds of personal, local efforts that are most effective. And, in the process, it has created "compassion fatigue," undermining Americans' traditional commitment to help those in need.

By turning responsibility for welfare back to the people, to local governments and to the states—along with the resources the federal government has been taking to support its failed effort—we believe America can, for the first time in many years, make real progress toward reducing poverty and providing opportunity for all her citizens. ★

CHAPTER FOUR

Cutting Subsidies

To the Privileged, the Powerful and the Elite

Glancing at this title, you might think it is about "the rich." Not so. While some of the privileged, powerful, and elite are wealthy, not all of them are, and it is not their distinguishing characteristic. What most distinguishes these groups is political power—the ability to influence the president and Congress to enact laws and spend money in their behalf.

For example, we never think of veterans as "rich," though some of course are. But veterans groups have enormous political power. The same goes for farmers, civil service retirees, sponsors of art organizations, and labor unions.

The American people are fed up with powerful interests controlling Washington, and they make no bones about saying so. Two-thirds of all Americans say Washington is so out of touch with America that it can best be described as an Imperial City that is run by an "Imperial Class." Who

belongs to that class? Eighty-nine percent say big businesses and corporations, 88 percent say lobbyists, 85 percent say the media, 82 percent say lawyers, and 69 percent
say unions.

The sense that Washington has been hijacked by
special interests has led to many of the recent phenom-
ena in American politics, from H. Ross Perot's success as
an independent presidential
candidate to passage of congressional term limit initiatives in twenty-two states. If
the new majority in Congress,
and the president who
promised to put "Main Street"
ahead of "Wall Street," want to
prove they are the reformers
they say they are, they can do
so by taking on the privileged, the powerful, and the elite
in both political parties.

> "There's no way
> for us to balance
> the budget. There
> are too many spe-
> cial interest groups.
> It's impossible."

In this chapter we offer our proposals to abolish or
reduce the benefits and subsidies of a long list of the privileged, the powerful, and the elite—the most comprehensive effort ever to take on Washington's special interests.
Some of the benefits and subsidies come in the form of
entitlements, some as direct federal grants, some as loans
or guaranteed loans, and some as tax preferences. Some
go to businesses, some to groups of individuals. Many of
them have a defensible purpose. But all the programs benefit relatively narrow groups of people while raising the
tax burden on the majority of people. In most cases, these
programs need to be simply and quickly eliminated. In a
few, the benefits can be spread more fairly and still save

the taxpayers a significant amount of money.

Our specific targets are:

★ Subsidies to farmers and agribusiness
★ Corporate welfare
★ Corporate tax breaks
★ Energy subsidies
★ Aviation subsidies
★ Amtrak
★ Excessive benefits to federal employees
★ Veterans benefits
★ National Endowments for the Arts and Humanities
★ Corporation for Public Broadcasting.

This is only a partial listing. A discussion of the complete listing of federal subsidies to special interests is too long for this book. More material on this subject can be found in Appendix Three.

SUBSIDIES TO FARMERS AND AGRIBUSINESS

Although spending on farm subsidies—which preceded the federal welfare system—is no longer as large a part of the federal budget as it used to be, it still ranks among the top spenders. It is also, as the polls tell us, one of the areas Americans are most anxious to cut. The time has come to make the first serious reforms in the farm subsidy programs' sixty-year history.

Every five years the farm programs are reauthorized by Congress, and every five years efforts are made to "cut" farm spending. But invariably the cuts are largely illusory.

The 1990 Omnibus Farm Bill, for example, was widely advertised as cutting about $11 billion from the current projections. Instead, actual spending in these five years (the final year's exact total is still not known) will be over $55 billion, not the $41 billion estimated. So what was advertised as a $11 billion cut (from $52 billion to $41 billion) *turned out to be a $3 billion increase!*

> **"T**he federal government should ask two questions: What's the original goal it intended to accomplish, and did it accomplish that goal? There has to be an internal review process. If a program isn't on target, either get it on target or get rid of it."

Farm programs are among the most complex in the government; they have a different subsidy system for each and every major crop grown in America. For that reason, some of our discussion of this topic appears in Appendix Two. But despite the complexity, several generalizations can be made:

★ Although Americans tend to think that farm subsidies mainly benefit the family farmers so dear to our national ethos, a large portion goes to big farming operations, many of them corporations. [See Figure 4.1] In one recent year, for example, 42 percent of the payments under the cotton and rice programs went to farms with incomes over $100,000. These large, profitable farms had an average income of $236,000 and an average equity (net worth) of $841,000. Furthermore, the wealthiest "farmers"—those with incomes of more than

$50,000—received federal farm subsidies even though they typically *received most of their income from non-farm sources, such as dividends and interest.* There is nothing illegal or even immoral about this, but it does shatter the mythology of the family farm. Recall the stories of farm subsidy payments going to celebrities like Sam Donaldson and to the well-off, non-tractor–driving residents of resorts like Marco Island, Florida.

★ The most costly farm subsidy programs guarantee farmers a price greater than what the market is willing to pay and thus encourage overproduction. Although this problem has lessened since the crisis of the mid-1980s— when Midwest grain elevators were literally overflowing—it is still a serious one, especially (as discussed in Appendix Two) in international trade negotiations, where our trading partners legitimately complain about subsidized American farm products competing unfairly

Figure 4.1

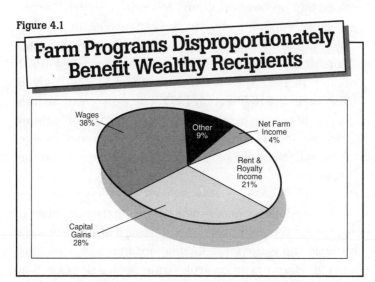

Farm Programs Disproportionately Benefit Wealthy Recipients

Wages 38%

Other 9%

Net Farm Income 4%

Rent & Royalty Income 21%

Capital Gains 28%

against their agricultural sectors.

★ The benefits showered on corporations and the rich are not the only inequity in the farm program. Different kinds of farm products receive wildly different levels of subsidies for no apparent reason. (Sometimes the subsidies are given directly, through federal spending; in other cases, they are transferred through limiting imports or otherwise curbing supply—programs that do not cost the government directly but do raise prices to consumers.) Rice producers, for example, receive a subsidy of over 50 percent of their prices, whereas soybean producers get only about 5 percent.

★ Although farm spending is down from its peak in the 1980s, reining it in could still result in large savings in federal spending. Spending for farm income stabilization in the three-year period 1992–94 averaged $12 billion a year.

★ Spending on farm programs has proved wholly unpredictable, varying widely from year to year. In a single year, the budget category called "farm income stabilization" doubled—from $12 billion in fiscal year 1984 to $23 billion in 1985. It then fell to $9 billion in 1990, only to rise again to $16 billion in 1993. The wide yearly swings occur because spending depends crucially on unpredictable factors like the size of the crops and foreign demand, that is, on such capricious unknowables as the weather.

These wild swings provide the rationale, if there is one, for government involvement in agriculture. Changes in supply can cause large fluctuations in prices, which no individual farmer can control. While we are skeptical that these conditions are any different, in principle, from the relatively wide swings that take place in other markets (real estate, for example), a case can be made that farming is "different." And a case can certainly be made that many family farmers today have made their plans with a reasonable expectation that the government will continue to help insulate them from year-to-year fluctuations.

> **"It's not so much a question of what we subsidize, but whom we subsidize. We've got a problem on our hands when we're giving our subsidies out to big business."**

What we propose here is to try out a new and radical approach to stabilizing farm income called "revenue insurance." Developed by a group of Iowa farmers, it is sometimes referred to as the "Iowa Plan."

Under revenue insurance, a farm's total revenues in a "normal" year would be calculated, and then the government would write an insurance policy assuring the owner of the farm some portion of that revenue. There would be a maximum amount of insurance per farm, set high enough to insure a large portion of normal revenues for the average family farm but a much smaller portion of revenues for the large corporate farms. Prices for the various crops would be freed from any government support, and deficiency payments based on the amount produced would end. The farmer would be insured against disastrously low prices or output, which was the problem that led to the government farm programs in the first place.

We need not go into all the detailed calculations here. One reasonable version of revenue insurance would save

$5 billion a year compared with the cost of continuing the present commodity programs. This is the approach we will incorporate in our budget estimates.

CORPORATE WELFARE

Farm subsidies are not, of course, the only federal programs that benefit corporations. You can find some form of corporate welfare tucked away in just about every corner of the federal budget.

As with the other programs that help the privileged and the powerful, federal subsidies to individual businesses or groups of businesses had a plausible reason at the start—usually to induce corporations to do something in the "public interest" that they would not do on their own. We shall simply list here some of these subsidies, all of which can be done away with in our effort to shrink government and balance the budget:

★ Export–Import Bank loans to promote exports
★ Road-building in national forests by the Forest Service to enable private timber companies to log the forests
★ The Rural Electrification Administration, which has long since achieved its goal of bringing electricity to rural areas and now subsidizes the power supply of large towns
★ Loans and guarantees of the Overseas Private Investment Corporation, which tries to induce American firms to invest in low-income countries
★ The Agriculture Department's "market promotion program," which subsidizes the advertising budgets of large American food companies in overseas markets

★ Sematech, a subsidy to develop machinery that makes computer chips

★ Subsidies to the automobile industry to help these companies develop a "clean" car

★ The Maritime Administration, which still subsidizes the voyages of some American shipping companies

★ The Industrial Technology Service of the Commerce Department, which helps American businesses apply new technology and supposedly become more competitive

★ The lending programs of the Small Business Administration, which have never served more than a tiny fraction of the millions of smaller businesses in the nation.

This list is not all inclusive, but it shows the many facets of subsidies for business. All can and should be ended.

CORPORATE TAX BREAKS

Abolition of special tax preferences would show up in the budget as increased revenues rather than reduced spending. As the reader knows, a major purpose of our plan is to *reduce*, not increase, the total federal tax burden. This overriding objective does not conflict, however, with the desirability of ending the many types of corporate welfare that are given out through the tax code rather than through direct subsidies.

Many of these tax preferences had a plausible reason for being included in the tax code, which is why the industries concerned were able to persuade Congress to enact them. But in some cases the original reasons no longer apply, and, in any event, a tax subsidy is not necessarily warranted just because it seems reasonable and plausible. Presented below are some of these tax breaks and their cost to U.S. taxpayers:

★ Oil and gas tax breaks: The famous depletion allowance and the fast depreciation writeoffs (called intangible drilling costs) in the oil and gas industry can no longer be justified. There is plenty of profit to be made from striking oil without tax breaks. If oil exploration activities should decline a little because the tax preferences are eliminated, it would not be a national tragedy, despite the sincerely held belief of the oil industry to the contrary.

The revenue gain from this change would be little over $1 billion a year.

★ Tax breaks that subsidize inefficient production, particularly in the energy area: These include the alternative fuel production credit, the enhanced oil recovery credit, the new technology credit, and the alcohol fuel credit. These provisions subsidize particular fuels, favoring one energy source over another without regard to economic efficiency. They have had no noticeable impact on the nation's basic energy balance sheet, and as noted below, there is no energy "crisis" to warrant such subsidies.

The revenue foregone from these subsidies through the tax code is about $1.2 billion a year.

★ Tax preferences that favor parts of an industry over others: Examples include the exemption from tax of credit union income (not granted to banks and savings and loans) and certain insurance industry tax provisions such as the small life insurance company deduction.

The revenue loss is a little over $1 billion a year.

★ Tax preferences that subsidize "politically correct" investments: The deferral of tax on gains from the sale of broadcasting facilities to minority-owned businesses, repealed by Congress in early 1995, is a good example of this. Other examples are the tax preferences for clean-fuel-burning vehicles and properties, tax incentives for the preservation of historic structures, incentives for rehabilitation and construction of low-income housing, and special rules favoring Employee Stock Ownership Plans.

The revenue loss from this list is nearly $5 billion a year.

★ Tax exemptions in the *federal* revenue code for certain *state and local* bond issues that are not general purpose bonds but rather help to finance essentially private activities: These include industrial revenue bonds of various kinds, bonds to finance private housing, and bonds for airports, docks, stadiums, and convention centers. These provisions subsidize state and local efforts to use public resources to compete against each other for new business development or to provide particular benefits to particular groups. There is no national interest involved.

The revenue loss from these exemptions is more than $4 billion a year.

ENERGY SUBSIDIES

The nation, deluged in ominous predictions and warnings from Washington, came to believe in the 1970s that there was an "energy crisis." There wasn't and isn't. But the widespread belief that a crisis did exist led to a variety of government subsidy programs to develop such things as solar and other forms of "renewable" energy. The government also launched an effort, now costing nearly $400 million a year, to create energy from fusion—the energy source of the hydrogen bomb. After twenty years, it is clear that fusion holds little promise of useful benefits for the next thirty to fifty years—if ever.

If there is to be research in the field of energy, including fusion, it should be carried out by the National Science Foundation, competing against other research outfits for the available funds. There is no need to make a special case of energy. The United States, like nearly every other country, imports a sizable portion of its energy supply, particularly petroleum, but this is no cause for alarm. We have always depended on imports of some things, from coffee to manganese. Energy is not different, just bigger. And there are abundant and diversified world sources of supply.

Cutting unnecessary energy subsidies would produce annual savings of nearly $5 billion.

AVIATION SUBSIDIES—PRIVATIZING THE FEDERAL AVIATION ADMINISTRATION (FAA)

Commercial airlines and private pilots make up another group that benefits, without justification, from federal largess. Because existing user fees do not fully cover the cost of providing flight control services, every takeoff and landing drains the federal Treasury. Additionally, every year the FAA provides airports with grants for expanding capacity and improving terminals.

We propose to privatize the FAA, a proposal that has been made by others, including the Clinton administration. There is no convincing reason why commercial airlines and private pilots should be subsidized by U.S. taxpayers. A privatized FAA would charge large enough fees to be self sufficient and make a profit. And, unlike the current FAA, it would have both the freedom and the incentive to upgrade its outmoded technology and hence make air travel both safer and more efficient. The increase in airport traffic suggests that airports would have little trouble paying their operating expenses through landing fees and financing capital improvements by issuing bonds to the public.

We estimate the annual savings from this proposal at just over $2 billion annually.

AMTRAK

Americans have a certain nostalgia for the passenger train. But nostalgia is not enough to justify the nearly $540 million in operating subsidies for Amtrak in 1995 alone, and hundreds of millions more for future capital improvements. Amtrak is going deeper and deeper into the red, despite more than $13 billion of subsidies since 1971. The General Accounting Office recently concluded:

It is unlikely that Amtrak can overcome its problems in financing, capital improvements, and service quality—

and continue to operate the present nationwide system—
without significant increases in passenger revenues and/or
subsidies from federal, state, and local governments.
Continuing the present course—maintaining the same
funding level and route system, even with the proposed
cuts in service—is neither feasible nor realistic because
Amtrak will continue to deteriorate.

It is not as if Amtrak is a low-income subsidy program. More than half of the riders earn incomes of more
than $30,000 a year, according to passenger surveys. The
average subsidy per passenger per ride on Amtrak is more
than $30. The nation's train passengers, thanks to this fed-
eral government bounty, are among the privileged, making Amtrak a kind of middle-class welfare.

But it is also a very selective form of middle-class
welfare. It has been argued persuasively that Amtrak's
current routes have more to do with congressional committees than with economic sense or consumer demand.
Amtrak's routes travel through precisely the states they
must travel through to gain sufficient political support in
Congress to continue the program.

The truth is that if Amtrak should cease to exist, the
nation's passenger transportation system would hardly
feel the difference. Amtrak represents less than one-half of
1 percent of the total intercity passenger mileage.
Compared with the automobile, the airplane, and the bus,
the passenger train is an anachronism.

We propose that the government acknowledge failure and close out Amtrak and its subsidies, along with several related rail passenger subsidy programs. Commuter
trains may make sense in some localities, but if so, they
should be subsidized locally, not by Washington.

EXCESSIVE BENEFITS
TO FEDERAL EMPLOYEES

Since 1980, federal civilian employees have received wage and benefit increases *four and a half times* larger than private sector workers, and they receive benefits far more generous than their private sector counterparts.

Federal employees have "earned" these generous benefits the old-fashioned Washington way: They lobbied for them. Government employee unions are among the largest contributors to political campaigns and, with nearly a million members in the four main federal unions alone, they provide perhaps the largest single source of campaign workers. Union representatives are active, especially within the Democratic party, where the head of the largest public employee union is also a member of the Democratic National Committee.

Government workers are much maligned, often unfairly. As individuals, they are for the most part hard working and conscientious and just as frustrated about being trapped in unworkable bureaucracies as the people are at having to deal with them. But the fact is, when benefits are included they make more for comparable jobs than the taxpayers who are paying their salaries. That's not fair, and the proposals below would go a long way to bringing the system back into balance.

FEDERAL RETIREMENT PROGRAMS

It is entirely proper for the federal government, a large employer, to have a pension plan for its employees,

military and civilian—just like any private employer. The
problem with the federal program is that, in at least two
respects, it is far more liberal than nearly all private plans.
And this is costly to the budget: federal retirement programs, civilian and military, will pay out $70 billion in
1995.

Federal retirement programs are generous in good
part because, as in the case of veterans and a few other
groups, federal employees are a powerful voting bloc with
members in every congressional district. There is no
inherent reason that retirement benefits should be so liberal, particularly now that federal salaries have become
more comparable with private pay for similar occupations.

The element of the federal retirement program that
most distinguishes it from nearly all others is that it provides *an automatic cost-of-living increase every year for the
retirees*. Such a feature would be far too costly for private
employers to include in their pension plans. In addition,
the federal program starts retirement benefits at a com-
paratively young age.

To reform federal pensions we propose to base our
plan on the changes recommended by the Concord
Coalition, headed by former Senators Paul Tsongas and
Warren Rudman:

★ Cost-of-living (COLA) increases would be eliminated for
   the younger retirees, those aged sixty-two and younger.
   At age sixty-two there would be a one-time "COLA
   catch-up" payment, and thereafter retirees would
   receive partial COLA's every year.
★ Pensions would be calculated on the basis of the average
   of the highest four years of salary for civilian workers,

instead of the highest three used at present. For military retirees the pension would be based on the highest twelve months of salary rather than the salary at retirement. These changes would slightly reduce the basic pension amount, but the pensions would continue to increase year after year because of the COLA feature.

★ Federal workers also have the option of a savings incentive plan like the 401(k) plans offered by private employers. Here again, the federal employer matching payment is quite generous in comparison with private plans. We propose that the federal government continue to match the first 1 percent of pay contributed to the plan by the employee, but above that level the federal match would be reduced to 50 cents for each dollar contributed.

These changes would leave federal employees, civilian and military, with an excellent pension plan, though not quite so generous as now.

The savings under these proposals would be nearly $6 billion by the year 2000.

FEDERAL EMPLOYEE
HEALTH BENEFITS

The federal government provides not only a pension plan for its employees but also—again like many companies in the private sector—a choice of health plans. As with many private companies, the government and the employee both make contributions to the health insurance plan that is selected.

The health plans offered by the federal government

are not excessively generous to the employees. But there is strong evidence that the plans are making unnecessarily high payments to doctors and hospitals. Various studies suggest that the federal employee health plans may be paying about 54 percent higher doctor fees than the fees fixed under the Medicare program, and about 43 percent higher hospital fees than the Medicare schedule.

Our proposal, again following the suggestion of the Concord Coalition, is to require that federal health plans limit their payments to doctors and hospitals to the amounts allowed under Medicare. The savings to the federal government would be about $2 billion by the year 2000.

VETERANS BENEFITS

No one would deny America's veterans the benefits they were promised and deserve for the sacrifices they have made to keep America free. But veterans, like public employees, represent a powerful political force, and they have used that power to win some federal subsidies that most people don't believe make much sense. Moreover, the federal government, fearing the anger of veterans groups, continues to run a system of hospitals exclusively for veterans—hospitals that often provide substandard care at an above-standard cost. In cleaning out the underbrush of unnecessary federal spending, we must address several relatively minor aspects of our veterans benefit programs.

The array of veterans benefits includes free health care in Veterans Administration hospitals, education benefits, and two cash benefit programs—compensation payments for disability and "pensions" for poor elderly veterans. The pension program is small, has not been increasing, and will gradually decline as veterans of World War II die. We propose no change in that program. We do propose a modest change in the veterans compensation program, now costing $14.5 billion a year, in which benefits based on disability go to rich and poor alike.

Few people begrudge veterans compensation for their service-related injuries, especially injuries incurred in combat. But payments also go to veterans who, while in the service, suffered injuries when they were on leave and off the base. They also go to veterans who incurred, while in service, such common ailments as heart disease, diabetes, osteoarthritis, and other diseases that occur in the population at large and have nothing to do with military service. Data collected by the VA indicate that compensation for these disabilities costs approximately $1.5 billion annually. In addition, compensation payments go to veterans with minor disabilities such as flat feet. About 1.3 million veterans are getting benefits of $71 to $170 a month though they are rated 30 percent disabled or less.

Again following a suggestion of the Concord Coalition, we propose to phase out over the next five years compensation payments for veterans whose disabilities (1) are not related to their military duties and (2) are less than 30 percent disabling.

We also believe that the veterans hospital system has outlived its usefulness. In a society where most people have health insurance (which was not the case when the VA hospitals began), there is little reason for a large special hospital system for veterans, which will cost more than $16 billion in 1995. The entire system of VA hospitals needs to be privatized and merged with the rest of the

American health care system. But since such a transition will take many years, we propose a series of reforms for the short run that should save almost $600 million in the first year and significantly more, about $2 billion, when fully implemented. These include:

★ Closing or converting hospitals that are notoriously inefficient
★ Phasing in the Medicare "prospective payment" system of establishing the cost of each treatment
★ Making a better effort to collect from private health insurance companies, where relevant, including making available to the Veterans Department the information on private insurance possessed by the Medicare program
★ Increasing cost-sharing for long-term care.

All these changes will be politically difficult. But challenging the politically powerful is an essential part of the effort to shrink the Washington government.

NATIONAL ENDOWMENT FOR THE ARTS AND HUMANITIES

This item arouses more passionate feelings than almost any other. It is true that government support for the arts and humanities has a long history, going back at least to Florence during the Renaissance. But it is also true that the United States, for most of its history, had a flourishing artistic enterprise—painting and sculpture, theater and ballet and opera, literature of all kinds—long before federal government support for the arts and humanities began in the 1960s. The end of federal support, as part of the indispensable shrinking of the Washington government, will not leave Americans starved for artistic activity, as the opponents of any change often argue.

The principal support for the arts has always come, and still comes, from ticket revenues, private donations, and local government support. Federal funds have undoubtedly been useful to some artistic organizations and others in the humanities, but they are not vital. Moreover, the (frequent) sheer foolishness and (occasional) outright offensiveness of some of the individual grants are familiar to all—and illustrate why having the government in Washington acting as an arbitrator of what constitutes "good art" is a bad idea on its face.

CORPORATION FOR PUBLIC BROADCASTING (CPB)

The case for a subsidy for public broadcasting has been greatly weakened by the explosion of cable TV channels. For example, it is very hard to distinguish—in quality and seriousness—the historical programs on The Learning Channel or the wildlife programs on The Discovery Channel from comparable programming on public television.

Except for the occasional big hit like the series on the Civil War, public television has always had a very small share of the viewing audience. And while it may not be fair to call its audience the "elite," it is certainly not Bubba or Joe Sixpack. Certainly, the spending practices of its management and contractors are not plebeian: frequent trips on the Concorde to Paris and London conferences, lush receptions, and multicourse banquets are a regular staple for the powers that be at CPB and their friends.

"Barney" will not disappear, children, if the nearly $300 million annual federal subsidy for public broadcasting dries up. Rather, CPB will be forced to operate more like a business, and those who benefit from watching it will have to pay for what they are getting.[1]

SUMMARY

The foregoing is a partial listing of federal programs that benefit the privileged, the powerful, and the elite, which we feel can be abolished or reduced. A few of these programs are entitlements, but most are "discretionary"— i.e., they can be reduced or terminated by Congress simply by denying them funds in the annual appropriations bills.

Representative Robert L. Livingston of Louisiana, the new chairman of the House Appropriations Committee, coined a useful phrase to describe some of these federal subsidies. He called them "nice-to-haves." Some of the activities we describe above we would oppose as a matter of principle—subsidies to business and others that the government should not be handing out under any circumstances. Others we would acknowledge are "nice-to-haves," but they are not essential.

The People's Budget calls for a dramatically smaller government in Washington, and while it might be "nice to have" some of the programs listed above, it will be just as nice not to pay taxes to the government in Washington to support them. ★

---

[1] It is worth noting that "Barney" alone has annual revenues (from licensing and product sales) of over $800 million

CHAPTER FIVE

Sending It Home

Restoring the Tenth Amendment

The Tenth Amendment to the Constitution, adopted as part of the Bill of Rights, reserves to the states all powers not explicitly granted to the federal government. The vast array of federal grants in aid to the states that has sprouted in recent decades, from education to highways, does not violate the letter of the Tenth Amendment, but it certainly violates its spirit.

As we noted in our discussion of block grants in Chapter Three, there is something illogical about federal grants to the states. It is all taxpayers' money, after all—some of it borrowed money, in the federal case, but still "ours." To state or local governments, Washington seems to be an endless cornucopia of funds, and they constantly pressure Congress for more and more grants to avoid having to raise taxes themselves. But it all comes out of the American people—either more federal taxes or more debt.

We do not propose to end all federal grants to state and local governments right away, but we do intend to reduce them now and eventually end most of them. There are different reasons for changing the present system—and somewhat different proposals—in individual programs. But all have the same fundamental defect: They make federal taxpayers pay for local programs, giving the illusion that somehow the programs are "free" when they are not. It is important to remember that the sweeping proposals for a smaller Washington government in the People's Budget will make significant federal tax reductions possible, and this will open up tax resources for the states to use if they want to spend in particular areas.

Specifically, we propose to end, or dramatically reform, federal spending in:

★ Education
★ Job training
★ Highways
★ Mass transit
★ Human development programs
★ Water and sewer grants
★ Housing-related grants

Every one of these areas is appropriate for some form of government intervention. Indeed, some are at the very core of what government is supposed to do. But should the *federal* government run your schools, decide where to build your roads, subsidize your bus fare, or help lay your sewer systems? Most people don't think so, and we agree.

EDUCATION

Thirty years ago, as the explosion of federal programs under President Johnson's Great Society initiative was just warming up, federal spending on elementary and secondary education—that is, aid to the public schools— was less than $1 billion, most of it under the long-standing federal program of aid to local vocational schools. The education of children in the public schools was regarded as entirely a local responsibility, sometimes with aid from the state government.

The American people still long for education to be handled locally. In a *Wall Street Journal*/NBC News poll conducted in December 1994, 72 percent said states should be given more responsibility, compared with only 22 percent who wanted more responsibility for the government in Washington. Americans feel more strongly about keeping education under state control than about any other federal program.

Although federal involvement in elementary and secondary education began at a modest level, by 1995 federal spending had risen to *nearly $16 billion*. (It still accounts for only about 7 percent of total spending on the public schools.) We readily acknowledge what is evident from polling data—that the American public is not niggardly when it comes to spending on education, which rightly is seen as the road to a better future for the nation's children; people tend to favor more spending on education, not less. But in the case of the federal spending, a serious question arises, what has it accomplished?

Looked at in one way, federal spending would appear to have been *counterproductive*. The dismaying decline in

Figure 5.1

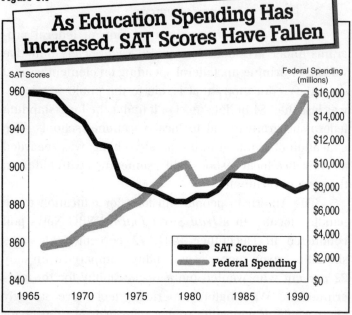

As Education Spending Has Increased, SAT Scores Have Fallen

the educational achievement of American children—so well documented in recent years and summarized in the famous 1983 report, "A Nation at Risk"—began in the late 1960s, just about the time President Johnson and Congress launched the first major federal aid to education. [See Figure 5.1] We do not claim that federal aid *caused* the deterioration in educational standards and achievement, but it certainly did not make American educational performance any better.

The main program at the very beginning was called, in government jargon, Title One (now Chapter One). It was supposed to concentrate federal aid on school districts with high proportions of "educationally disadvantaged" children (though in fact some aid under this program goes to almost every school district in the country). It has grown steadily and amounts to $7 billion in 1995. There could be no better indictment of the failure of Chapter One than that made by the Clinton administration itself (which nevertheless supports Chapter One and wants to increase it). The president's budget for 1995 had this to say about the Chapter One program:

> National evaluation studies by independent groups and the Department of Education document that Chapter One and other Elementary and Secondary Education Act programs have had little impact on the educational progress of the 5 million children served, despite expenditure of tens of billions of dollars over the years.

The administration's answer, of course, was to "restructure" the program "to produce better results," and Congress did enact a few cosmetic changes in 1994. Our answer in this as in other areas is to stop pretending that programs can work when they clearly have not worked, with decades of effort to prove it. Indeed, Chapter One has had from the beginning a perverse incentive: the school districts that could show that their children were the dumbest got the most money!

"I think education—or lack of a decent education in this country—is the biggest obstacle to the American Dream."

Federal aid to elementary and secondary education, so widely hailed when the first bill was enacted under President Johnson, has been a failure. It has given states

and local school districts more money—and created a lot
of paperwork and bureaucracy—to little purpose. But
while many individual programs can and should be terminated, an abrupt cutoff of all federal aid would pose difficult problems for local school
systems.

**"It's all appear-
ances. We have the
highest graduation
rate, because we
graduate kids who
can't read."**

We propose to consolidate
Chapter One and a few other
programs into a new interim
block grant, reduced by 10 percent from the combined total of
the programs that are included.
We would terminate a group of
ineffective smaller programs
totaling almost $1 billion, in-
cluding such items as "professional development grants,"
"arts in education," "instruction in civics," "magnet schools
assistance," and "women's educational equity." The very
names of these education programs suggest what is wrong
with federal aid to education and with grants to the states
in general: once the Pandora's box has been opened, every
member of Congress with a pet cause wants to create a
special grant program to foster it. The interim block grant
would itself be terminated by the year 2000.

Federal aid to higher education—primarily grants or
loans to individual students to enable them to go to college—is another matter altogether. Starting with the GI
Bill of Rights after World War II, which enabled several
million veterans to get a college education, federal student
aid has had a generally successful record. This is so
despite various problems and abuses, including ripoffs of
the system by fly-by-night vocational schools of various

kinds and the emergence of a class of deadbeat former students who do not repay their loans. There is nevertheless a clear public purpose in student aid. Making available a college education to a deserving student who otherwise could not afford it is an enormous benefit not only for the individual but for society at large.

Thus we believe that the basic program of guaranteed student loans, along with Pell grants for the neediest students, should continue. Guaranteed student loans are, in effect, a public subsidy to individuals to help them attain a college degree. We do not quarrel with the principle of a subsidy, only with its magnitude.

At present a student is charged no interest on the loan as long as he or she is in college. It makes good sense to delay the payment of both principal and interest on the loan until after graduation, when the student begins to earn an income. But, given the huge lifetime benefit of a college education in terms of increased income, it is entirely reasonable to charge interest on the loan from the time it is made.

While interest would accrue during the time the student is in college, no payments would be due until after graduation. One effect of this change would be to give college students who use subsidized loans a little more incentive to complete school on time or even early. And when they do graduate, the effect of the change would simply stretch annual payments on the loan out over time—but not increase them.

JOB TRAINING

As in the case of education, the American public

instinctively supports the concept of public spending to
improve work skills. Again like education, job training is
seen as a road to a better future and higher income. In
addition, a case can be made that otherwise highly desirable federal policies—freer trade through reduced import

**"The programs—
the mechanism—to
make job training
work are just not
there."**

barriers and closing defense
bases, for example—indirectly
cause people to lose their jobs,
which creates an obligation on
the part of the federal government to help them acquire new
or improved skills.

In assessing the twenty-
five-year federal effort at job
training it is important to recognize at the outset that most
training is, and always has been, provided by employers
and fellow workers in the workplace. The vast majority of
our working people have found jobs and improved their
skills *with no participation in federally financed job training programs nor even any awareness that they exist.*

Spending on federal job training programs—the
General Accounting Office counted 163 of them—now
amounts to about $7 billion a year (the Clinton adminis-
tration also counts $6 billion of Pell grants to low-income
students for vocational-type college and junior college
higher education, making a total of $13 billion). The large-
ly untold story is that the achievements of all this federal
effort are slim indeed. This is particularly the case with the
subpopulation supposedly most targeted—disadvantaged
youth and young adults. In the past twenty-five years,
when federal job training spending rose from $1.6 billion
to more than $7 billion, the disparity in wages and salaries

between the poorly educated and those with more education has grown significantly. *Job training was supposed to narrow it by giving those with limited education job skills and thus higher wages.*

One way or another, most of the poorly educated are getting jobs, simply because the demand for labor has grown with the growing economy. Federally financed training has made little difference, though it has undoubtedly raised the skills of some people. As further evidence of the irrelevance and inefficacy of federal job training programs, there has been no improvement over these twenty-five years in the dispiriting and long-standing two-to-one disparity between black and white unemployment, even when the total unemployment rate declines. Once again, this is precisely the kind of disparity that job training was designed to reduce.

As in the case of federal educational programs, the best indictment of the federal job training maze comes from the Clinton administration itself. The following is from the president's 1996 budget:

> The many programs, with their conflicting rules and administrative structures, confuse the people they are intended to help, add bureaucracy at every level, and waste taxpayer money.
>
> Not surprisingly, states and localities complain about the problems of coping with so many different federal rules and reporting requirements.
>
> In many programs, bureaucrats make choices about jobs and training for individuals, as if individuals cannot choose for themselves; nor is the private sector plugged in enough to help. . . .
>
> The quality of training and related services is uneven,

and the programs often do not require accountability for
results; institutions continue to get federal funds regardless
of performance.

In the case of job training, we want to give the president credit for proposing an aggressive set of reforms
(although he and his secretary of labor, Robert Reich, want
actually to *increase* the amount of federal money spent on
job training). We adopt many of the principles of their proposals as part of a transition phase. But we believe these
programs have demonstrated a record of failure sufficient
to justify their ultimate termination. Specifically, under the
People's Budget:

★ The present maze of programs would be abolished and
  the money for the principal ones would be consolidated
  into a block grant going directly to the states with little
  federal involvement. Most of the federal job training
  bureaucracy would be abolished.
★ The states would make most of their job training grants
  directly to individuals, in the form of training vouchers.
  The individual could select his or her own job training.
★ The amount of the block grant would be 50 percent of
  the combined total of all the present programs.
★ At the end of a five-year transition phase, in the year
  2000, we would end the block grant and return responsibility for worker retraining programs entirely to the
  states.

HIGHWAYS

The federal government got involved in road-building in a big way for the first time in 1956, and for a good reason—to build a new system of interstate superhighways to link all of the state capitals and other major cities. The interstate system was a legitimate federal public works project.

That was forty years ago. Then a funny thing happened. The superhighway system got built, finished, completed—but federal aid to highways went on. It amounts to nearly $20 billion in 1995.

The money is now used, among other things, to *maintain* the interstate highway system, though the original premise of the proposal by President Eisenhower and the legislation passed by Congress was that the federal government would build the new roads but each state would maintain the segments within its borders. Again we have the fundamental flaw of grants in aid. Since the states felt that the federal money was "free," they soon persuaded Congress to pay for maintenance, particularly as the new interstate system began to wear out.

When the American people are asked about spending money on roads and transportation, their answer was clear: 70 percent want the responsibility to rest with states and local governments, while only 22 percent want to involve the federal government. Next to education, highways are the program Americans most want to see returned to the states.

As we all know, the bulk of federal aid to highways is paid for by the earmarked federal gasoline tax, now 14.1 cents a gallon. Once the hurdle of imposing the tax was passed, there was no problem maintaining and even increasing it and then doling out the money to the states.

Earlier, we proposed to terminate the gasoline tax,

along with other excise taxes, in order to provide a tax base for the states. Here, we propose to terminate the federal programs the gas tax supports.

Our proposal for highways is very simple. End the pork barrel aspects of the program—called "demonstration" grants for particular road projects—immediately. Then terminate the accompanying highway grant program by the year 2000, and let the funding and the decision-making for maintaining the highways go back to the states.

The interim proposal would reduce new federal spending on highways by roughly $3 billion annually.

MASS TRANSIT

Several presidents have tried to scale back significantly the big federal subsidy program for local subway and bus systems, but to no avail. These grants will cost almost $4.5 billion in 1995.

Numerous studies have shown that new subway systems fail to reduce traffic congestion and pollution, yet they cost billions. Ridership estimates are often far too high. Moreover, federal subsidies for mass transit have been a bonanza to the transit unions, which have won wage levels far higher than those prevailing in their areas for similar skills.

Local transit systems should set fares at a level that will cover costs. There is no reason for South Dakota farmers to subsidize, through their federal taxes, New York subway riders. No strategy for shrinking the Washington government worthy of its name would fail to terminate mass transit grants, and we propose to do so—right away.

HUMAN DEVELOPMENT PROGRAMS

This is a catchall name for various types of "social services." Some of the federal programs are already in the form of block grants that resulted from the consolidation of separate programs. These include the big Social Services Block Grant, the Community Development Block Grant, and the Community Services Block Grant. Other programs include low-income energy assistance, payments to the states for child care assistance, preschool funding, nutrition assistance, maternal and child health, and substance abuse grants.

We propose to terminate some programs, including low-income energy assistance (a creature of the "energy crisis" of the 1970s. We would consolidate the rest into a single large interim block grant. As with other block grants, we would reduce spending 10 percent below the 1995 level to reflect the reduction of federal administration and mandates. Then, as in the case of the above programs, the grants would end in the year 2000.

WATER AND SEWER GRANTS

This federal program grew out of the Clean Water Act, the first of the major environmental statutes. Up to that time water and sewer systems had always been (and mainly still are) a quintessentially local responsibility. Because the Clean Water Act required a big new investment in sewer systems, the case was made for an "interim" system of federal grants to local sewer systems. But, as usual, it never went away. Washington has spent more than $60 billion overall and is now spending nearly $3 billion a year. The more money the federal government has put in, the less has been spent by state and local governments, so that the net effect has been to move control of the programs farther away from the people without necessarily improving water quality.

We would end this program right away and hence save nearly $3 billion. In some places, the federal money has been used to create "revolving funds" that use receipts from local sewage systems to finance new projects. These could, of course, continue, but no new federal grants would be made.

HOUSING-RELATED GRANTS

Along with the subsidized housing programs, discussed in Chapter Three, a series of grants programs to states and local communities related to housing has sprouted. They include the HOME housing investment partnerships, emergency shelter grants, and homeless assistance grants; states or cities can fund them if they are deemed a good use of taxpayer money. (States and cities can also use grant funds for these purposes, and housing assistance will, in any case, be provided to those in need through housing vouchers.) These grant programs, totaling about $2.5 billion in 1995, should be terminated.

CONCLUSION

The time has come to grasp the bull by the horns and see federal grants to the states for what they are—an illusion of free money. If there is to be public spending, taxpayers must pay for it; none of the money is free. Ending federal grants—along with lowered federal taxes—will not end public spending, but it will be financed where it should be—at the state or local level.

We have shown that some of the major federal grants haven't worked, and others have continued long after their original purpose was achieved. The time has come to end them, with interim block grants in most cases to provide for a smooth transition. ★

CHAPTER SIX

Transforming Medicare

And Saving It from Bankruptcy

Medicare, the government system that provides health insurance for nearly 40 million elderly and disabled Americans, is in terminal crisis. The program's costs are increasing at such an unsustainable rate that Medicare stands to bankrupt not only itself but the entire federal government as well. Indeed, unless Medicare is reformed, it will soon begin to hurt the very citizens it is supposed to protect. As Lonnie Bristow, M.D., president of the American Medical Association, said in January 1995:

> If you heard a giant screeching on New Year's Day, it was the sound of a paradigm shifting. On January 1, 1995, the first Baby Boomer became eligible for membership in the American Association of Retired Persons. At first it's going to be just a trickle, then it'll become a torrent, and before we know it, they'll all be racing toward 65. And

when they get there, the first thing they're going to ask for
is their Medicare card. But at the rate we're going, they
might not be able to get one—unless Medicare is
changed—changed dramatically and changed definitively.

> **"This isn't about bureaucracies.**
> **We're not just talk-ing about money.**
> **This is health here.**
> **We're all concerned about costs and all that. If we don't look out, Medicare could end up taking all our money."**

The problem with Medi-
care can be thought of in two
parts. First, in the short run, the
system is literally approaching
bankruptcy. According to the
trustees of the Medicare trust
fund, it will run out of money
within seven years.

Saving Medicare from
bankruptcy does not require
"cutting" spending—spending
will continue to grow rapidly.
But the short-run reforms proposed here will nevertheless
cause screams of pain from
every health care interest group
in Washington—especially hos-
pitals and doctors, who currently make large profits from
the system and want to keep it that way. They will work
hard to scare not only senior citizens with talk of Medicare
cuts, but also members of Congress, and they will hire the
best lobbyists, pollsters, and advertising agencies to protect
their interests.

The second part of the challenge is to transform
Medicare from a 1960s-era bureaucracy to a 1990s system
offering consumer choice—a people's health care system
that puts individuals in the driver's seat where they can

make decisions for themselves. Fortunately, things are already happening in medicine that will help. Technology is enhancing the opportunity for people to control more of their own medical care and to limit the explosion of costs. A proliferation of books, magazines, and CD-ROMs provide details about illnesses, drugs, and treatment that once only doctors could access. New medical testing devices, moreover, free people from constantly making trips to see the doctor (already people can test their own cholesterol, blood pressure, and pregnancy, and they soon will be able to do home AIDS testing).

The demand by consumers for more control over their health care, and the technology that is fostering this trend, run directly counter to the inevitable momentum of the current Medicare system—increasing command and control by the federal government in a desperate effort to halt the program's mounting costs. Reversing that trend will require changing the system. That is what we propose.

> **"The [health care] debates scared me. They scared me, because I could see my coverage being questioned every day. I was afraid that all of a sudden, poof!—the dust would settle and my old insurance would be nowhere to be found. But from what I understand, that's what's going on with our money anyway— someday in the near future, the dough is just not going to be there."**

THE EXPLOSION OF MEDICARE SPENDING —AND THE MYTH OF CUTS

Medicare costs are growing at 10 percent annually. To reform the program we must address the main source of growth—the increases in the volume and intensity of medical services. Surprisingly, longer lifespans and the rise in the number of elderly have been responsible for only about 15 percent of Medicare growth, while the increasing price of services accounts for about 25–30 percent of it. Most of the growth lies elsewhere—in the volume, type, and intensity of services.

One thing is for certain, without reform the system will soon be bankrupt. The trustees of the Medicare trust fund reported in April 1995 that the trust fund would be exhausted by 2002, [See Figure 6.1] and the two public trustees—the ones who don't work for the government—issued a statement declaring that "the Medicare program is clearly unsustainable in its present form." They added that "Medicare reform needs to be addressed urgently."

Currently, it takes four workers to pay for each Medicare beneficiary. But early in the twenty-first century, as the baby boomers retire, it will be down to only two workers for each recipient. The hospital part of Medicare (called Part A) is financed by a payroll tax on all employees. (The Medicare tax is lumped together with the Social Security tax as a payroll deduction.) These taxes are paid into a trust fund—but the trust fund will soon pay out more in Medicare benefits than it receives from payroll taxes, and thus it will run out of money by 2002. That's seven years from now. Taxes can be increased on workers only so much before they revolt.

Figure 6.1

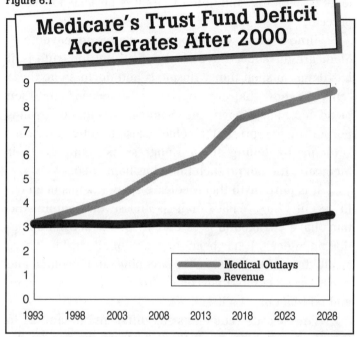

Medicare's Trust Fund Deficit Accelerates After 2000

Legend: Medical Outlays, Revenue

X-axis: 1993, 1998, 2003, 2008, 2013, 2018, 2023, 2028

Y-axis: 0–9

Medicare's other program, Part B, the doctors' part of Medicare, is paid for partly by the elderly themselves (about $46 a month this year, normally through a deduction from their Social Security checks) but mainly through a direct subsidy from the general taxpayers, most of whom do not even realize it. Part B is growing even faster than Part A, and it is 70 percent subsidized by the general taxpayer.

In simple dollar terms, Medicare's cost increases are staggering. In 1967 it cost $5 billion. This year it will cost $176 billion—thirty-six times more than when it began. Between 1985 and 1994, a ten-year period, Medicare *doubled* in size. Currently, Medicare is almost 12 percent of all federal spending, and in ten years it is projected to be 18 percent.

Almost every year, Congress claims to have "cut" Medicare to reduce the budget deficit. But the truth is, it has done no such thing. Hospitals and doctors cite these "cuts" to show that they are being "squeezed," and then plead for higher payments. Some unscrupulous groups purporting to represent the elderly also frighten their constituents by telling them Congress is "cutting" their Medicare, though no such thing has happened.

It is pure myth that Medicare spending has been cut in recent years. What Congress and several administrations have engaged in is essentially budgetary manipulation and deceit. It has been the worst of all worlds. There is all the political pain—the weeping and wailing and gnashing of teeth—that comes from cutting a program, and no real cuts at all!

The word "cut" has a different meaning in Washington double-speak than it has in the rest of the country. To most people, a cut means to reduce spending from what was spent the previous year. In Washington, a cut has come to mean that you increase spending, but less than you projected. This "baseline budgeting" allows politicians to claim they are cutting spending while actually increasing it. In the case of Medicare, the "baseline" itself is artificial, which makes the problem worse.

On January 5, 1987, for example, the president's budget for 1988 was released. It proposed to restrain the growth in Medicare from 10 percent to 8 percent annually. The next day, the American Association of Retired Persons, the American Medical Association, the American Nurses Association, and the Federation of American

Health Systems ran a full-page ad in the *Washington Post* that read: "During the past 5 years, more than $30 billion has been cut from Medicare and Medicaid. Now the Administration wants to cut $50 billion more. Isn't it time we started defending the homefront?"

The ad was deceptive. Against the current baseline, or projected spending increases, Medicare and Medicaid had indeed been cut. Yet, in actual dollars spent, Medicare and Medicaid had increased by 1981 to 1986 by 71 percent. Nobody's medical services had been reduced at all.

We can expect to see many such ads in the current political season. As the new Congress attempts to slow the rate of Medicare growth from 10 percent to, say, 6 percent, the defenders of the status quo, despite the impending bankruptcy of the Medicare trust fund, will decry what they will call the "devastating" cuts. Only in the strange language of Washington could such a charge be made. (This phenomenon is not, of course, limited to Medicare. See the discussion of farm subsidies in Chapter Four.)

PRESCRIPTION FOR REFORM
(AND SOLVENCY)

Reform is clearly essential. But how should we reform? The answer is obviously not by following the cost control strategies of the last fifteen years, which have failed to stem the rapid growth in Medicare spending. Past reforms were primarily targeted at controlling the price of medical services paid by the government to doctors and hospitals. But this approach does not address the fundamental problem in the program: the growth in the volume and intensity of medical services used by Medicare recipients. As the government tried to control Medicare costs by limiting what it paid doctors and hospitals for each specific procedure, health care providers responded by increasing the services so they could regain lost income resulting from the price controls.

> "All I know is that I went in for a basic checkup, and the next thing I knew, they had me hooked up to so many wires and cables and meters that I didn't know what hit me. Pretty serious business to get rid of a bit of the flu."

To be sure, some of the growth in services that are provided stems from expensive new treatments. But the current incentives of the medical system, particularly in Medicare—where most patients pay no out-of-pocket costs even when consuming more services—are to overutilize new as well as old technology.

The only way to get control over the problem of the growth in volume and intensity of services is to create incentives for providers and beneficiaries to use medical services more efficiently. These incentives must be designed to shift most of the current burden of controlling the volume and intensity of medical services from federal rules and regulations—which have failed—to the private sector.

Costs can be controlled if it is in the interests of medical care providers—and consumers—to control them. This is already happening in the nongovernment part of the health care system. It will work in Medicare, too, and without harming the program's elderly beneficiaries.

Indeed, the long-run transformation of Medicare we are proposing will provide the elderly with more choices and higher quality care at a lower cost than if the system were allowed to continue as is.

The American people have already "reformed" the part of the health care system they control. In the private sector, several new approaches are having dramatic results in slowing the growth of costs while providing greater choice:

★ Medical Savings Accounts (MSAs), which allow people to have their own tax-free accounts to pay for routine care, while providing a "catastrophic" (i.e., high-deductible) insurance policy to pay for any serious illnesses

★ Coordinated care networks to control costs by better management of patient care and with greater emphasis on prevention

★ Bundling reimbursement for medical services into one payment to require the provider, instead of the insurer, to determine the appropriateness of services (when payments are made for each service separately, it is very difficult for the insurer to monitor their necessity and appropriateness)

★ More cost-consciousness among patients. If patients are

> **"When the government gets involved a bureaucracy grows so large, so fast that most of the money goes toward supporting the bureaucracy, not health care itself. It's just that I want to pay doctors, not bureaucrats."**

required to pay at least something for medical services,
they will be less likely to use unnecessary services.

These are the approaches the private sector—i.e., the
American people acting on their own—has taken to
improve medical care. The federal government should
adopt the same changes for Medicare. They will slow substantially the rapid growth in Medicare costs and, at the
same time, provide a wide range of health care choices for
Medicare beneficiaries. These choices include the traditional Medicare fee-for-service programs and Medicare
health maintenance organizations (HMOs), along with a
new Medicare preferred provider system. In fact, when
Americans are asked if they would be willing to join an
HMO or other coordinated care plan to help bring down
the nation's health care costs, almost three out of five (58
percent) say yes.

THE MSA OPTION

Perhaps the fastest growing and, over the long run,
most promising private sector reform for health care
financing is the MSA. As applied at a growing number of
companies, the plan works like this: Rather than getting
"first dollar" (or low-deductible) health insurance coverage from your employer, you get a high-deductible "catastrophic" insurance policy to cover major illnesses. And
you get something else—a check, usually for an amount
equal to or just slightly less than the deductible on your
insurance policy. The only catch is, the check is deposited
in a special account which—for the first year—can only be
used to pay for medical care. This MSA account ensures

that you have money to pay for routine doctors' visits or other relatively small bills not covered by your high-deductible insurance policy. But when the year is up, you can take any money left in the account and use it as you wish.

Not surprisingly, the MSA concept provides a dramatic incentive for people to (1) stay healthy and (2) ask how much things cost before they buy them. And, because people pay their own bills for their routine care, they save a tremendous amount of money by not running every expense through the cumbersome (and annoying!) insurance reimbursement system. In the growing number of companies that are offering MSAs as an option to their employees, the results indicate that people like them (80–90 percent of employees choose the MSA option), that they save money for the company, and, perhaps most important, that most people who choose the MSA option have money left in their accounts at the end of the year.

It is interesting to note how rapidly the MSA concept is spreading when you consider that MSAs suffer a major disadvantage in the tax code: Although employer payments for insurance coverage are fully deductible (neither the employee nor the employer pays any taxes on them), contributions to MSAs are considered "income" and are thus subject to Social Security taxes (over 15 percent for both the employer and employee share) and, when employees take the money out, subject to income tax as well!

Because Medicare recipients are virtually all retired, the MSA concept cannot be fully implemented within the Medicare program. But a variant on the MSA concept is one of the options that can and should be part of the trans-

formation to a more choice-oriented system. The plan
would work as follows:

★ **First,** Medicare beneficiaries who choose the MSA
option would no longer pay the Part B premium—currently $46.10 each month. They could keep this money
and do with it what they choose.

★ **Second,** Medicare would pay for a high-deductible
insurance policy (say $3,000), which would ensure that
beneficiaries who suffer serious illnesses or hospital
stays would be covered against major expenses.

★ **Third,** Medicare would also deposit money into the beneficiary's MSA account, which could be used to pay for
routine care, or to buy supplementary insurance or
insurance for long-term care. Although the amount
deposited into the MSA would not fully cover the
deductible, funds would be allowed to accumulate, so
that nearly all beneficiaries would soon have balances
in their accounts greater than the deductible under the
"catastrophic" policy.

THE COORDINATED CARE OPTION

Another major change sweeping through the private
health care sector is the growth of HMOs and other coordinated care providers. Traditionally, doctors and hospitals
were paid for each service they performed. Coordinated
care providers, by contrast, are not paid per service, but for
the complete care of an individual. Today, one-fifth of
Americans—more than 50 million people—are enrolled in
coordinated care programs (generally HMOs), and the
growth continues dramatically. Between 1992 and 1994,

nine million people joined HMOs.

Medicare is running far behind the times. Indeed, as shown in Figure 6.2, only about 7 to 10 percent of Medicare beneficiaries are enrolled in HMOs. As the program is currently structured, beneficiaries have no incentive even to consider HMOs. Since most of today's elderly grew up before HMOs came on the scene, they see no reason to switch from their current fee-for-service providers.

But HMOs are an option worth considering. Because they do not get paid more for performing more tests and services, they give doctors and hospitals an incentive to

Figure 6.2

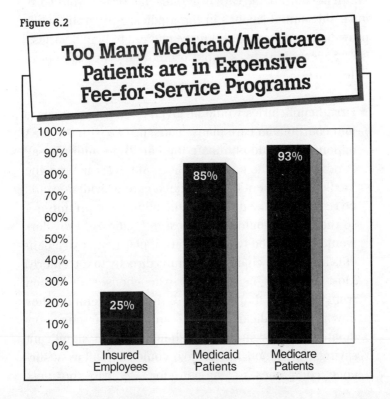

limit those that are unnecessary. Health care costs are controlled. Equally important, people in HMOs are as satisfied, and in many cases more satisfied, with their care as
those in fee-for-service plans.

As HMOs come to compete, many will offer lower
prices to get more business. But they also compete for
their enrollees on customer service. As long as they are
competing against other health care providers on an even
playing field, they cannot offer substandard medical services and continue to exist.

Creating incentives for Medicare beneficiaries to
enroll in coordinated care programs like HMOs would produce substantial savings in the Medicare program, while
providing quality care and more choices to beneficiaries.

Several initiatives could promote the use of coordinated care.

★ **First,** beneficiaries would be given greater incentives to
join coordinated care plans. Thus, just as with the MSA
option, we would eliminate the Part B premium for all
beneficiaries who join such plans. At the same time, the
Medicare payment to coordinated care providers would
be reduced by the amount of the eliminated premium—
so that there would no net cost to Medicare. Providers
would be allowed to offer different plans and extra benefits and would charge premiums directly to the elderly.
Most Medicare beneficiaries who choose this option
would pay less than the $46.10 monthly premium they
now pay to Medicare. In fact, competition among coordinated care organizations should lead to significant
savings for beneficiaries. (We could also allow insurance companies to compete for Medicare business

under this option.)

★ **Second,** to encourage competition, coordinated care providers could elect to reduce the standard payment they receive from Medicare. For each dollar less that Medicare paid to the provider, its members would receive 50 cents from Medicare. Thus, if the provider were to accept $400 less per beneficiary from Medicare than the standard payment, each beneficiary would receive a check from Medicare for $200.

★ **Third,** the Medicare system would offer coordinated care providers the option of either receiving an annual payment—which might fluctuate from year to year, as it has in the past—or receiving a guaranteed payment rate for three years. Providers that chose the three-year guarantee would be certain of payment, in return for which they would forego one percentage point of the regular annual increase in the Medicare payment.

THE FEE-FOR-SERVICE OPTION

Having offered these very attractive options for Medicare Part B, we believe that the current fee-for-service program should also be an option for those who choose it. But they should understand that the current system is dramatically more expensive than the other options being offered, and if they want it, they should pay more to have it. Under the fee-for-service option we propose, future beneficiaries becoming eligible for Medicare as they reach age sixty-five could still choose a fee-for-service plan, but they would pay a higher premium—$20 a month more than the present premium. While this change would not take effect until 1998, it would be announced now, as part of the reform legislation, giving those who will soon retire an opportunity to consider all the options and make an informed choice.

(Why not have everyone join a HMO or purchase insurance through an independent insurance company? If Medicare were being started anew, this flexible and freedom-of-choice system would most likely be instituted, rather than the bureaucratic behemoth we now have. But the elderly have become used to the present system. Moreover, even though the system must be changed, it cannot be done overnight. The current system must be retained as an option, at least during the transition.)

FREEDOM OF CHOICE

All of these options would be made available to Medicare beneficiaries through an open enrollment season like the one offered to federal employees and in many private companies. Each year, Medicare beneficiaries would be given a comprehensive package of materials that inform them about the various options, from MSAs to coordinated care to fee-for-service plans. They would receive information about HMOs in their geographic area and about other companies (e.g., insurance companies) offering coordinated care packages.

Thus, a transformed Medicare would offer freedom of choice. Medicare beneficiaries could choose insurance that best suited their needs. They could join an HMO, obtain insurance through another plan, select the catastrophic/MSA option, or stay in the Medicare fee-for-service system, depending on what premiums they are willing to pay.

INTERIM REFORMS

Transforming Medicare will not happen overnight. Most current Medicare beneficiaries are likely to stay with the current fee-for-service system.

Thus, to save Medicare from impending bankruptcy, we propose a series of reforms of the current system. A complete discussion of these reforms—which are about as arcane as the system itself—can be found in Appendix Two. Briefly, however, we would:

★ Create a preferred provider organization (PPO) within Medicare, similar to what Blue Cross/Blue Shield and other insurance companies have done. Under a Medicare PPO system, doctors and hospitals that chose to participate would agree to accept discounted payments and monitor their volume of services

★ Apply Medicare's prospective payment system of cost control to post-acute care services (e.g., skilled nursing, rehabilitation, home health), which are currently exempt from this.

★ Reduce Medicare payments for physicians on hospital medical staffs that consistently perform more tests and procedures than the national median, to give doctors in these hospitals a direct incentive to control costs.

★ Reduce Medicare payments to hospitals with excess bed capacity. Medicare capital payments would be based on actual hospital occupancy as opposed to assumed occupancy.

★ Adjust the Medicare Part A deductible (downward) and the Part B deductible (upward) to reflect the fact that the Part B deductible has not been subject to cost-of-living adjustments from the very inception of the Medicare program, while the Part A deductible has (and hence is much too high relative to the Part B deductible). This will lower costs of those with the more serious and expensive illnesses that are covered by Part A's hospitalization insurance.

★ Continue the approximately $5 increase each year in the Part B premium that has been enacted by Congress in each of the last three years.

★ Include home health visits and laboratory services in the Medicare co-payment program, so that beneficiaries pay part (between 5 and 20 percent) of the costs.

★ Maintain the annual increase hospitals receive under the prospective payment system at the current levels to reflect the true increase in their costs, after productivity increases, and make other adjustments to avoid overpayments to many hospitals.

To reiterate: these proposals will produce howls of pain and accusations of unfairness from the medical industry, and it will try to scare both the elderly and the politicians. But we believe that most Americans understand how anachronistic and inefficient the current centralized system is. Moreover, enough people have experienced the benefits of greater choice in their own health care decisions to support the transformation we are proposing here. Still, the fight over Medicare, in 1995 and probably for several years to come, will be perhaps the most difficult fight the American people will have to wage against defenders of the current status quo.

For those who want to save Medicare and see lower taxes and a balanced budget, the fight is an important one.

The reforms proposed in the People's Budget will not cut Medicare, but they will slow the rate of growth below its current, unsustainable level. Coordinated care, particularly HMOs and PPOs, are reducing cost growth in the private sector and should do so in Medicare. Increased cost sharing, as described in Appendix Two, will reduce growth directly, through reduced payments by the government, and indirectly, through providing disincentives to overuse medical services.

Anyone who claims he or she is able to predict with precision the effect changes of this magnitude will have is fooling himself or herself. Indeed, past projections of much smaller reforms have proven notoriously unreliable. But we believe the reforms proposed in the People's Budget will dramatically reduce growth below its current level of 10 percent, to a range of as low as 5 percent or as high as 7.5 percent. To err on the side of caution, we

Figure 6.3

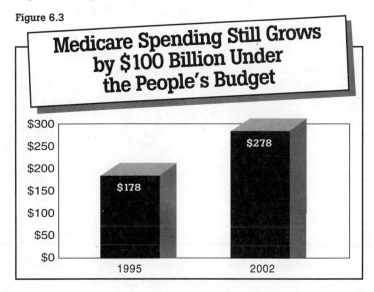

Medicare Spending Still Grows by $100 Billion Under the People's Budget

assume that, between now and 2002, annual growth will average 6.5 percent. That would be a big change from the current situation, but spending on Medicare would still grow from its 1995 level of $178 billion to about $278 billion in 2002. [See Figure 6.3] ★

CHAPTER SEVEN

Reforming the Pentagon

*Revitalizing America's Defenses
and Cutting Foreign Aid*

Protecting the nation is the primary responsibility of the federal government. The American people want to know that our armed forces can respond effectively to foreign threats—and win.

The end of the Cold War led to a level of optimism about international politics not seen since just after World War I. A "new world order" would, it was said, permit radical disarmament and huge reductions in defense spending. As it turned out, that optimism was only partly justified. Although America's last great military rival—the former Soviet Union—is no longer a "clear and present danger," the world is still a dangerous place.

In the global village of the 1990s and the coming century, conflicts in lands once considered remote can have real and immediate implications for the U.S. economy and security. The impact of a local disorder can place an entire regional economy at risk—with consequences that can spread throughout the world trading system.

It is also true, if frightening, that efforts to contain the spread of weapons of mass destruction are having only limited success. Many nations, and even terrorist groups, are able to acquire the weapons and delivery systems needed to attack the continental United States.

America's ability to project its military force to protect its vital interests was a tremendous source of national pride when, in 1991, U.S.-led forces defeated Iraq and forced Saddam Hussein out of Kuwait. That success was due in large measure to the technological edge American forces enjoyed, especially in information technology and "intelligent systems." Such systems have revolutionized warfare, and they will continue to do so. For American forces to be able to prevail in the future, they must maintain their technological edge by continuing to adopt information-age systems.

In a Luntz Research poll conducted of 1,000 people nationwide between February 22 and 23, 1995, 79 percent of Americans responded that it is still important to modernize our military forces, despite the end of the Cold War, while just 16 percent stated that modernization is not important. While the end of the Cold War did not eliminate the need for a strong defense, it did eliminate America's largest and most threatening rival. As a result, we can afford to spend less on defense and still know that we can protect our national security.

The People's Budget proposes a total of $1.3 trillion

in defense spending over the course of the next five years—roughly $20 billion more than the Clinton administration's plan, but less than what many Republicans in Congress have suggested. Budget authority will not increase for the first three years, while outlays will actually decrease. (Outlays represent the amount of cash paid out each year. Congress appropriates budget authority annually, and the authority produces outlays over several years.) As with domestic discretionary spending, we will reform first and then allow modest growth of the programs that remain. The end result is to leave defense spending at less that 3.5 percent of the GDP, or less than half the share of national income spent on defense during the 1980s.

But this modest level of spending is made possible only by dramatic reforms in both how we spend our defense dollars and what we spend them on. In this chapter, we propose fundamental reforms in the defense bureaucracy, in the Department of Defense's (DOD's) outmoded methods of procurement, and in its personnel policies. And we propose to end the practice of using the defense budget as a hidden source of support for social programs. Over the next five years, these proposals will save nearly $90 billion when compared with the budget proposed by the Clinton administration.

At the same time, we believe that additional spending is needed to keep America strong. Our armed forces are not purchasing enough of the current generation of weapons nor are we developing the new weapons systems that will ensure our continued technological superiority. (While defense spending, adjusted for inflation, has fallen by one-third since the peak year of 1987, defense procurement has been reduced at twice that rate.) Thus, we propose to redirect the $90 billion saved through reform—plus an additional $20 billion—to ensure that America has a strong enough military to maintain its leadership position in the world.

This chapter also includes a brief discussion of foreign aid—a small but controversial part of the overall budget. The American people oppose foreign aid by wide margins, and in most cases they are right. We propose to cut the foreign assistance and other international affairs program in the budget by $4 billion next year and to eliminate four international affairs bureaucracies that are no longer needed.

Additional details on both the defense and foreign aid proposals are contained in Appendix Two.

REFORMING THE PENTAGON

Despite all the rhetoric to the contrary, the Pentagon is in many ways still the same Cold War bureaucracy it was in 1989 when the Berlin Wall fell. Its failure to implement thoroughgoing reforms prevents it from using the appropriated funds to modernize our forces in order to exploit Information Age technologies. While almost everyone recognizes the need for reform, thus far the reforms have been few in number and have had little effect on the cost of defense.

Although the international scene has changed fundamentally, there has been little change in the management of defense resources. The DOD maintains a unique procurement system that has resisted more than a decade of reformist rhetoric and legislation. While civilian personnel have been reduced along with military personnel, core central activities such as depot maintenance have not been reformed. The leadership has made statements about the importance of exploiting commercial products and practices in place of the existing military acquisition system, but little real change has taken place. DOD is still overly dependent on the old Cold War defense industrial base (the "military-industrial complex")—especially the highly specialized producers whose knowledge of the DOD's unique cost-based procurement system provides a distinct, if unjustifiable, competitive advantage.

Excessive DOD overhead, such as unneeded military bases and facilities, has continued despite the political formula developed in the 1980s to bring the political deadlock over base closures to an end. Similarly, DOD's obsolescent practice of maintaining its own development and support infrastructure, when a parallel one is available at lower cost in the private sector, increases the total cost of buying and maintaining defense systems.

Policy choices also have an adverse impact on the cost of defense. The Clinton administration's decision to emphasize the United Nations as the primary institution for coping with international security needs has imposed a substantial financial load on the United States. To make these operations work, the United States has been forced to finance much of the costs (e.g., logistics support, intelligence communications, and the rest)—costs which are not, under UN rules, reimbursed by our allies. As one American told a focus group interviewer, "We might be a world superpower, but that doesn't mean we have to go around paying the military bills for the rest of the world."

Finally, having nondefense-related programs financed through the DOD has deprived the department of the resources needed to meet current and future security needs. The Congressional Research Service has estimated that the cost of nondefense expenditures in the DOD budget for fiscal years 1995–99 is more than $60 billion ($11 billion in FY 1995 alone).

The practices described above are bad defense policy *and* bad budget policy. We propose to change them. Specifically, we propose to:

★ Reform procurement procedures (five-year savings = $10 billion)
★ Implement management reforms such as privatization and closure of unneeded military bases (five-year savings = $13.5 billion)
★ Change the way some defense systems are paid for (five-year savings= $15 billion)
★ End the practice of using the defense budget to finance social programs (five-year savings = $50 billion).

Efficiency probably will never—and probably should never—be the first priority of the DOD. Its first job as we said, is to keep America safe. But until it becomes more efficient, until it changes from an inefficient industrial-age bureaucracy to a modern, efficient institution, Americans will be skeptical about spending additional money on defense.

The proposals we offer above would begin the

needed transformation. The changes we propose below show how the savings from those reforms should be spent to ensure America's national security, which today's shortsighted policies are placing at risk.

REVITALIZING AMERICA'S DEFENSES

When, following the collapse of Soviet military power in 1991, the public lost interest in national security affairs, it helped to obscure the drastic extent to which the defense establishment was being demobilized. Moreover, the diversion of resources needed to sustain both the short- and long-term ability of the armed forces to respond to twentieth-century military contingencies puts at serious risk the ability of future presidents to conduct an effective foreign policy and to cope with threats to American interests.

1. Develop/improve U.S. capabilities to cope with the consequences of the failure of current policy to contain the proliferation of weapons of mass destruction and their means of delivery.

2. Accelerate the modernization of U.S. military platforms and subsystems to leverage "information warfare" opportunities created by U.S. scientific and industrial leadership in underlying technologies.

3. Improve the ability of the United States to project power abroad from the continental United States or from forward deployed sites on a coalition or unilateral basis.

4. Refocus and modernize U.S. intelligence collection and processing and its command, control, and communication (C3) systems to support U.S. national security needs in the twenty-first century.

Revitalizing America's national defense means that important changes must be made in the Clinton administration's two recent budgets for FY1995 and FY1996. The above list describes the four areas where significant improvement in our defense capabilities are needed.

Respond to the Threat of Proliferation of Weapons of Mass Destruction

The collapse of the former Soviet Union has magnified a frightening problem: the growing ease—economic, technical, and political—with which technologies and materials can be obtained to build weapons of mass destruction. The existing multilateral controls (i.e., the Nuclear Non-Proliferation Treaty for nuclear weapon technology, the Australia Group for chemical weapons, and the Biological Weapons Convention) are proving less and less effective. As a result, twenty-five nations either already have or are developing the capability to build (or buy) and operate ballistic missiles capable of attacking the United States and weapons (chemical or nuclear) capable of killing large numbers of American citizens.

Most Americans believe that we have at least some defense from a ballistic missile attack. But, in fact, no such defense exists—not even against a single nuclear-armed missile aimed at an American city.

More than a decade after President Reagan launched the Strategic Defense Initiative, the government has spent approximately $30 billion developing antimissile defense systems. Thanks in part to that research, there are today affordable approaches to providing an antimissile defense system. All that is required is the incremental upgrading of systems already being deployed.

But the Clinton administration's policy of continued adherence to the Anti-Ballistic Missile Treaty (ABM) of 1972—supported by many on both sides of the aisle in Congress—limits the ability of the United States to exploit these low-cost options to defend the nation from cruise and ballistic missile attack. It also prevents us from sharing this technology for defense with allies such as Israel, Japan, the Republic of Korea, and the Republic of China (Taiwan).

The ABM treaty is a Cold War relic that has outlived its usefulness—indeed, it has outlived one of its two signatories, the Soviet Union. Continuing to abide by its provisions is preventing America from defending itself against a real, immediate, and growing threat. This policy ought to be changed.

When the Strategic Defense Initiative ("Star Wars") was launched, effective missile defense was a hope for the future. But a mere decade later, there is nothing futuristic about defending America against a limited attack. Indeed, an effective near-term system can be created by making use of the inventory of U.S. Navy *Aegis*-class ships and upgrading their radars, signal processing, C3, and interceptor missile complement to engage the full range of ballistic missile threats—short, intermediate, and long-range. If we employ the technology that permits maximum use of on- and off-board sensors and interceptor performance, it would take only a few of these ships to provide coverage for the entire United States against at least modest attacks.

Accelerate U.S. Military Modernization

The current system of defense resource allocation has virtually halted most near-term platform (i.e., weapon delivery system) modernization initiatives. Programs such as the F-22, a new strike aircraft for the Navy, the Army's M1A2 upgrade, and similar platform modernization initiatives have been seriously delayed or reduced to little more than token efforts. Slowing up the introduction of more modern platforms and truncating next-generation research means that our armed forces will be ill-equipped to exploit the revolutionary civil sector technology that has created a new dimension of military power: information warfare.

The importance of information warfare developments is laid out in a recent work by Alvin and Heidi Toffler *(War and Anti War)*: the conduct of a nation's warfare parallels the manner in which it creates wealth. The pervasive impact of civil sector information technology by the civil sector promises revolutionary changes in military effectiveness with radically smaller force structures. By employing a complex of sensors, signal processors, telecommunications systems, and advanced computation, U.S. forces will be able to operate inside a potential adversary's decision cycle and defeat his means of power projection, C3I, and mobility.

While it is beyond our scope to explain here, the application of information warfare concepts and technology will be critical to American security in the twenty-first century. Unless we proceed, this widely distributed civil technology will eventually be acquired by our enemies and employed militarily. The U.S. military needs to speed up its modernizing efforts in the following areas:

★ Tactical aircraft (e.g., F-22, naval variant of the F-117, F-16 replacement, F-15 upgrades)
★ Sensor/C3 improvements and force structure augmentation (e.g., AWACS upgrade, JSTARS force structure increase, MILSTAR, Army/Navy C3 enhancements, etc.)
★ Strike systems that provide precision attack and damage assessment at great standoff ranges against the full spectrum of targets
★ Conversion of major ground and naval force platforms to digital electronics to permit "seamless" integration of all service elements in future military operations
★ Intelligence collection and processing to permit timely transmission of target data to the appropriate platform/weapon system.

The Clinton administration's admirable effort to accelerate the introduction of commercial products, technologies, and practices has been marred by its slow implementation. Technologies needed to accomplish these objectives are available in the civil sector, but the failure to allocate adequate resources to do this has delayed American forces from being able to reap the benefits of American scientific and inductive leadership.

Improve U.S. Power Projection

The diversity of future threats in both geographic and military terms requires highly flexible and effective power projection capabilities. These capabilities need to be very flexible so that they can be employed by an ad hoc military coalition in response to the formal mandate of, say, the UN or on a unilateral basis. Power projection has been a central feature of American defense policy throughout its history. The realities of the post-Cold War period increase the importance of U.S.-based power projection to augment operations arising from forward deployed ground, air, and naval forces. Among the critical power projection initiatives that need to be funded are:

★ Worldwide nonnuclear CONUS-based aerial strike capability, which includes sustaining the B-52 force, converting the B-1 to a conventional strike role, and sustaining the B-2 production line
★ Increased acquisition of the C-17 strategic airlift aircraft to support a one-for-two replacement of the existing C-141 inventory, and acceleration of the modernization of the intra-theater C-130 inventory
★ One additional carrier battle group because the need for a post-Cold War forward military presence (despite a sharp reduction in land-based deployments) is inconsistent with the reduction in aircraft carrier battle groups. The ships, including the carriers, already exist. An additional battle group will shorten the currently lengthy tours at sea and thus improve retention rates for naval personnel.

Refocus U.S. Intelligence Collection and Processing

Despite all the rhetoric since 1991, little has been done to initiate reforms in the intelligence system to make it responsive to the new national needs.

Intelligence collection and processing have been subject to arbitrary budget reductions that increase the likelihood that developments of a political-military and scientific-industrial character will take us by surprise.

Contrary to current beliefs, the collection of intelligence against Soviet-bloc targets was relatively straightforward. Although the Soviet system was among the most secretive, its structure, geographic location, and methods of operation were well enough understood to allow very specialized and highly capable systems to be employed successfully. The geographic, political, and institutional diffusion of the contemporary world order requires greater, not less, attention to the intelligence system. Intelligence is also a critical component of the larger concept of information warfare. A more "seamless" delivery of intelligence products to users is essential to reduce the time between collecting the data and using them.

We should stop diverting the resources of our intelligence collection system to support private sector international projects. The intelligence function should be employed by the federal government to support national security purposes and not encumbered by the plethora of purposes frequently proposed that are not germane to United States national security interests.

The defense revitalization outlined above, and described further in Appendix Two, is quite small and inexpensive compared with the buildup of the 1980s. Altogether, these proposals would require spending about $106 billion more than the Clinton administration proposes over five years. Of that, $88 billion will be paid for by the reform proposals offered at the beginning of this chapter. The remaining $25 billion will not be begrudged by the American people who understand the need for lean, efficient, and strong armed forces.

CUTTING FOREIGN AID

Foreign aid accounts for roughly two-thirds of what is referred to in the budget as the "International Affairs Function." The function also includes the Department of State and a number of lesser foreign policy agencies.

While much was made of the notion of the "peace dividend" at the close of the Cold War, the idea does not seem to have had much of an impact on foreign aid or in the State Department. Indeed, little has changed in the institutions, instruments, or budget levels of international affairs. Reductions in security-related support of our allies have been more than offset by big increases in spending for a broad social welfare agenda. There has also been a shift away from bilateral programs controlled by the American government in favor of multilateral programs run by organizations like the United Nations. Finally, institutions such as the Agency for International Development (AID), the Arms Control and Disarmament Agency (ACDA), the Peace Corps, and the U.S. Information Agency (USIA) persist although they have outlived their usefulness in their current form.

With modernization, the cost of foreign aid and other international activities, after a period of transition, can be lowered by about one-third.

Institutional Reform

The institutions financed through the international

affairs budget have met the new situation of the post-Cold War period not by shrinking but by adding programs, personnel, and resources. Large, complex, and increasingly autonomous entities nominally under the Secretary of State have become obstacles to rather than agents of modernization. Institutional reforms can produce $3 billion in administrative savings over the next five years.

Arms Control and Disarmament Agency

The end of bilateral arms control negotiations with the former Soviet Union was the obvious moment to reform the arms control machinery, a reform long overdue. The focus of arms control has shifted almost entirely from negotiation to implementation. As a consequence, ACDA as an organization has been marginalized. Reflecting its irrelevance, the Clinton administration has failed to fill the agency's senior management positions below deputy director. The U.S. government's most effective and high-profile counter-proliferation initiatives (ACDA's proclaimed post-Cold War mission) are being conducted by the Department of State and the Department of Defense.

Reduced from its preeminence as the "cavalry" of the arms control agenda, ACDA is now little more than a "horse holder" providing overlapping support to other agencies. Apart from a modest number of specialists, ACDA is redundant. Its residual useful functions can be transferred to the Department of State with considerable fiscal savings and great improvement in policy coherence.

ACDA's superfluous role has been recognized by

the Department of State, which has recommended that
ACDA's mission be absorbed by State. This sensible
reform was rejected by the administration, but it is
included in the People's Budget.

Agency for International Development
AID has been besieged over time by demands for
literally scores of contradictory objectives from the legislative and executive branches of government.

The primary objective of the U.S. foreign assistance
policy should be to ease the transition of developing
states from state-dominated economies to market-based
economies. Instead, the thrust of AID's programs has
been to reinforce the intervention of the state in the economic development process. No amount of reform will
solve this problem, because the underlying concept of
development assistance (DA), as currently practiced by
AID, is fundamentally flawed. Giving money to (or
through) foreign governments does not help policy
reform, has no effect on the recipient with respect to the
implementation of U.S. foreign policy objectives, and
provides no discernible long-run benefits for the citizens
of the countries receiving the assistance.

This is not to say that there is no positive role for
DA or other activities currently performed by AID (e.g.,
international disaster relief). Technical assistance to
help create a legal infrastructure for commercial contracts and to protect property rights can accelerate the
displacement of state institutions. But these sorts of
activities do not require sending large amounts of
money overseas. Very large savings can be made by dramatically reducing DA funding, abolishing AID as an

independent agency, and integrating its residual functions into the Department of State.

U.S. Information Agency

Separating USIA from the Department of State helped to implement our foreign policy when propaganda was at the cutting edge of American foreign policy. The Reagan-era USIA was able to help undermine the Communist states in a way that was often difficult for the Department of State to do directly. Today, the rationale for sustaining the USIA as an independent agency has largely evaporated, both because of technical changes and the collapse of the former Soviet Union.

The worldwide commercial telecommunications system has proven to be far more effective in transmitting information than government-dominated information organs. The facsimile machine, the Internet, amateur radio, and the modern international voice telecommunications system were crucial in such disparate events as the Tiananmen Square demonstrations and the Balkan civil war. The USIA, by contrast, has relied too extensively on low-efficiency forms of transmitting information and has not taken adequate advantage of the new technology that is widely available.

The isolation of the USIA from the rest of the foreign affairs institutions has led to a loss of coherence and a glacial pace of adjustment to post-Cold War realities. The continued independence of the USIA poses a threat to the coherence and effectiveness of U.S. foreign policy.

In short, the practice of multiple "independent" agencies within the foreign affairs network has created

significant difficulties in policy management at U.S.
diplomatic missions abroad and in Washington.
Restoring the information policy function to the
Department of State will permit the secretary and the
president to speak with one voice in a world where
information policy will be and must be managed with
finesse. The recommendation by the secretary of state to
disestablish USIA should have been accepted.

Department of State
The Department of State has earned a reputation
for being unable to manage its programs, services, and
facilities effectively. Years of bureaucratic growth, abet-
ted at times by congressional intervention, have made
the management of the department so top-heavy (more
than two dozen offices are headed by officials with the
rank of assistant secretary or above), that decision-making has become extraordinarily difficult.

The department has largely ignored numerous
high-profile management studies commissioned by various secretaries of state, the Congress, and senior subor-
dinates. These studies show that consolidating state
functions around the core regional and functional
bureaus would permit a 50 percent reduction in the
department's management structure while improving
the responsiveness of our foreign policy to American
interests abroad.

Program Reform
In addition to these institutional reforms, the
People's Budget proposes several major changes in U.S.
foreign aid policy that will result in a dramatically small-

er overall budget. The reforms proposed here (and detailed further in Appendix Two) include:

★ Cutting development assistance contributions to multinational organizations and limiting bilateral development assistance to helping other nations (especially the newly independent states of Eastern Europe) create market-based economies
★ Replacing some security assistance grants with loans, or guaranteed loans, and making foreign governments pay for their purchases of U.S. arms (when this is in the national interest) instead of giving them away.

Budget Savings

The changes proposed in the People's Budget result in a 16 percent reduction in spending in the first year. As the program is implemented, however, the savings go up, and by the year 2000, spending will be roughly one-third lower than it is today. ★

CHAPTER EIGHT
The Payoff

The People's Budget proposes the most complete transformation of the government in Washington at least since the Great Society:

★ The responsibility for running *and paying for* state and local programs would be returned to the states and localities, where it belongs—and where people can hold elected officials more accountable for producing results.

★ The government in Washington would be nearly one-third smaller, as a percentage of GDP, than it is today. At 15.7 percent of GDP, it would be the smallest it has been since 1951. [See Figure 8.1]

★ Most federal excise taxes would be eliminated and the income tax cut by 22 percent, giving people the funds to take care of themselves and their families and giving states and localities the tax base they would need to take on their new responsibilities.

Figure 8.1

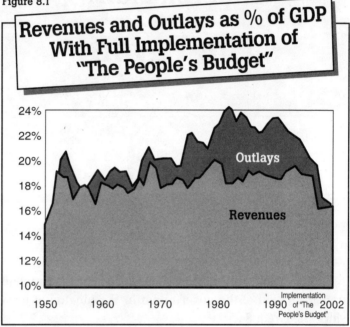

Revenues and Outlays as % of GDP With Full Implementation of "The People's Budget"

★ Medicare would begin the transformation from a 1960s "command and control" bureaucracy to a 1990s system of consumer choice.

★ The federal budget would be balanced, and the debt would begin to shrink rapidly relative to the size of the economy. With Medicare saved from bankruptcy and the budget deficit finally eliminated, the foundation would have been created to deal with the looming crisis in Social Security.

As shown in Figure 8.2, the federal government that would remain would be a very different institution from the one we have today. Social insurance programs

(Medicare and Social Security) would account for nearly half of all spending, reflecting the need to make good on current commitments and the beginning of the baby boom influx of new retirees.

Defense and interest on the debt would account for the next largest pieces, roughly the same proportion of spending as today. The Department of Defense would be a very different institution, however, spending money where the rubber meets the road instead of on unneeded overhead and bureaucracy. Interest on the debt is simply, unavoidably, going to be with us for many years.

The two remaining categories—"domestic discretionary" spending and "welfare and other entitlements"— would be dramatically smaller as a percentage of overall spending than they are today. The first category shrinks by virtue of eliminating programs that benefit special inter-

Figure 8.2

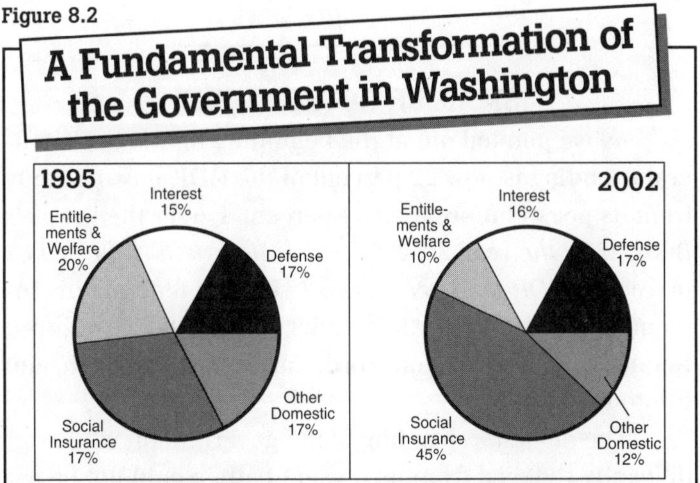

A Fundamental Transformation of the Government in Washington

1995

Entitlements & Welfare 20%
Interest 15%
Defense 17%
Other Domestic 17%
Social Insurance 17%

Total Outlays: $1.53 Trillion
Percent of GDP: 21.8%

2002

Entitlements & Welfare 10%
Interest 16%
Defense 17%
Other Domestic 12%
Social Insurance 45%

Total Outlays: $1.57 Trillion
Percent of GDP: 15.7%

ests or that would be better performed by state or local
governments and through the elimination of duplication
and overhead. But, crucially, the core functions of government included in this category—the Departments of
Justice, State and Treasury, for example—would be fully
funded to perform their functions effectively. As for
remaining entitlement programs, the government would
fund veterans benefits, federal employee retirement and
other essential spending.

In short, the government in Washington would be
"back to basics"—doing those things that are its to do more
effectively, with greater focus, while leaving to the people,
communities, and states the responsibility *and the freedom*
to perform the tasks that are rightfully theirs.

That, we believe, is what a people's government
ought to look like.

Here are the details.

_____

SMALLER GOVERNMENT

As we pointed out at the beginning of this book, federal spending is now 22 percent of the GDP, down slightly
from its peak of more than 24 percent. Under the People's
Budget, *by the year 2002 federal outlays will drop to 15.7
percent of GDP, the lowest since 1951.* The federal government would be smaller than under Presidents Eisenhower,
Kennedy, Johnson, Nixon, Ford, Carter, Reagan, Bush, and
Clinton.

The *domestic* spending of the government, while significantly reduced from its present path, would not be cut
as much as these figures suggest, because defense is so
much smaller, in relation to the economy, than it was dur-

ing the forty years of the Cold War. For example, in the year 1960, the last of Eisenhower's presidency, total domestic spending was 8.7 percent of GDP. Under the People's Budget, it will fall to about 13 percent by 2002. It will still be higher as a share of GDP than it was even at the end of Lyndon Johnson's presidency. Interest on the debt was a lower outlay then than it is now as a share of GDP, accounting for part of the difference. But even allowing for that, spending on domestic programs and activities after our reductions will be higher than in those earlier decades, largely because of the continuing growth of entitlements, such as Medicare and Social Security.

The smaller government that we offer is manifested in other ways as well. We propose to do away with four cabinet departments—Housing and Urban Development, Energy, Education, and Commerce (to be merged with the Department of Labor in a new Department of Commerce and Labor).

The Commerce Department is a misnomer. It is actually a collection of disparate activities—the Census Bureau, the Patent Office, the Weather Service, Economic Statistics—housed under one departmental roof. The activities that must continue, along with similar ministerial functions of the Labor Department such as administering the wage and hour laws, can readily be housed in one new department, at a considerable savings in overhead.

The Education Department was created under President Carter in the late 1970s on the mistaken assumption that what ailed American education could be fixed by the federal government. Almost two decades later it is clearer than ever how wrong that notion was. The Energy Department was another creature of the late 1970s, based on another mistaken assumption—that the nation faced an "energy crisis." It didn't and doesn't. As for HUD, it has, quite simply, failed in both its missions: to house the poor and to improve the cities.

While some activities of all of these departments will necessarily continue, the savings from abolishing them are still substantial. Under the item "Departmental Administration" for the Energy Department in the latest annual appropriation bill for the department was $281 million; for HUD, it was $451 million. Most of this money will be saved.

The reduction of the federal bureaucracy from our proposals will be substantial. It is important to note that a large number of federal employees are not bureaucrats in the usual sense of that word. They are Park Rangers and FBI agents, statisticians and meteorologists, diplomats and customs agents, U.S. attorneys and tax collectors. That is, they are doing jobs that the people want the government to do. But plenty of other federal employees are shuffling paper, and many of those jobs will go. We estimate the reduction of the federal work force at about one-fifth, or around 400,000 people—many of them from the top-heavy bureaucracy of the Department of Defense.

A special and important case concerns the recent bureaucratic miniexplosion in the government's regulatory agencies. Between 1988 and 1995, what the government calls the "full-time equivalent" work force in the regulatory agencies (excluding the banking agencies such as the Federal Reserve) grew by more than 22,000, or 23 percent of the 1988 staff levels. Some of this resulted from new statutory duties required by acts of Congress, but most represents more intensive regulatory activity under statutes that were already in place in 1988.

The growth has been concentrated in six agencies that regulate various kinds of private activity—the Coast Guard, Environmental Protection Agency, Fish and Wildlife Service, Food and Drug Administration, Securities and Exchange Commission, and Animal and Plant Health Inspection Service. We propose substantial reductions in staffing in all of these areas, though not in all cases back to the 1988 levels. More sensible and less intrusive regulation is of course one of the people's aims for the new majority.

Another way of describing the downsizing of the Washington government is to point out that, under our proposal, new funding for domestic discretionary spending (that is, nonentitlement spending) will be cut by 26.5 percent—more than one-fourth—over three years. And that is before the withering away of the new interim block grants in areas like education and job training after the year 2000. By 2002, domestic discretionary spending will be about $180 billion compared with today's $257 billion, even though many accounts will necessarily be allowed to grow modestly in the interim.

LOWER TAXES

The objective of our proposal, shrinking the government, has merit in its own right, as we explained in the earlier chapters. But it also makes possible a double bonus—elimination of the big budget deficit as well as lower taxes. Put another way, we have shown how to cut spending more than *just* enough to eliminate the deficit.

The first part of the tax reduction bonus has

already passed the House of Representatives as part of the
Contract with America. In our budget totals, we assume
these proposals will pass the Senate and be signed into
law. (Two relatively minor provisions for corporations,
involving a neutral cost recovery system and a repeal of
the corporate alternative minimum tax, are not included.
We have doubts about their economic merits and believe
these changes should be considered in the larger context
of tax reform, a topic that will soon appear on the political
agenda.) The tax reduction package includes a $500 per
child tax credit for families with incomes up to $200,000; a
reduction of the "marriage penalty"; a significant reduction in the capital gains tax to spur investment; a new type
of tax-favored savings account; an increase in the amount
of an estate that is free of tax at death; an increase, by the
year 2000, to $30,000 in the amount a Social Security recip-
ient could earn before losing any benefits; and several
other tax changes.

The additional reduction of federal taxes made possible by the shrinkage of government will make tax
resources available to the states as they assume responsibility for welfare. We suggest that the tax reduction should
take place in two ways.

First, we would eliminate most federal excise taxes,
including taxes on gasoline, cigarettes, alcoholic bever-
ages, and telephone service. The reason for eliminating
federal excise taxes is that these are the taxes most easily
and simply picked up by the states as they take on the burden of spending on welfare. The states will have plenty of
warning. They can enact in advance laws to assume some
or all of the federal taxes as they are terminated. The
change would not even be noticed by consumers.

Obviously, we are not seeking to tell the states what they ought to do by way of welfare spending or what federal excise taxes they should pick up, but we are suggesting a fairly painless way to ease the transition. This change would free up more than $40 billion in revenues now going to the federal government, which could be picked up smoothly by the states.

Second, we propose to cut federal income taxes by 22 percent, or $170 billion in the year 2000. (As noted in Chapter Two, the exact size of the income tax reduction will be established as the plan kicks in in the year 2000. It will depend on how the economy has been performing and on the progress being made toward a balanced budget.) This cut could be accomplished in any number of ways— by cutting rates across the board, increasing further the deductions for children and other dependents or creating a "flat tax." The point is that the federal income tax burden on taxpayers would be reduced by 22 percent.

Most states have income taxes (many of them "piggybacked" on the federal income tax), and, as with excise taxes, they could pick up rather simply what has been cut at the federal level if they want. Again, we are not suggesting what they should do but only demonstrating that revenue resources will be available to the states to match the new spending burdens they will assume. Because we believe that the states can more efficiently run these programs than the federal government, there should be a net reduction of the total tax burden.

Based on the conservative Congressional Budget Office (CBO) economic assumptions we have used and the spending reductions proposed in this book, the federal tax cut in 2000—excise taxes and income taxes—will be $212 billion, and it could well be significantly larger.

Given our focus on turning welfare back to the states, along with the revenues to pay for it, it is worth taking a moment to take another look at the impact of this shift on them. As shown in Table 8.1, our proposal would eliminate $258 billion in federal welfare spending. To compensate for this reduction in money from Washington, states would receive, first, $26 billion in compensation grants, targeted to the poorer states who would need the most help. Next, as discussed in Chapter Three, the federal government would create a tax credit for individual contributions to public assistance charities or to state or local government public assistance programs. If everyone took advantage of this credit, it would ensure an additional $40 billion to help the poor; and if the total tax credits claimed were less than $40 billion, the difference would be added to the compensation block grant. Finally, the federal government would cut income and excise taxes by $212 billion.

Thus, the federal government, by lowering its own taxes, ensuring private support of private charities, and

Table 8.1

Federal/State Tax and Welfare in the Year 2000

Reduction in Federal Grants to States	**$285 Billion**
Increased Revenue Available to States	
Federal Tax Cuts (Revenue Base Made Available to States)	$212 Billion
Federal Compensation Grants	$26 Billion
Tax Credit/Compensation Grants	$40 Billion
Total Additional Revenue Available to States	**$278 Billion**

creating a block grant for poorer states, would actually make available a total of $278 billion, $20 billion more than the $258 billion it would be cutting from federal welfare spending.

The real difference: instead of being dictated to by the government in Washington, the people and the states would now be deciding how best to use this money to promote opportunity and to help those in need.

A BALANCED BUDGET

The final element of the payoff is the achievement of the long-sought, elusive goal of a balanced budget and the beginning of a reduction of the huge national debt.

Before discussing the very real benefits of balancing the budget, we want to point out that *our spending and revenue estimates do not rely on any improvement in economic conditions as a result of implementing the People's Budget* (see Appendix One). We use the conservative economic assumption of the CBO, the most important feature of which is their assumption of 2.3 percent annual economic growth. We do not assume higher economic growth and hence higher revenues—even though cutting taxes will almost certainly create more growth. Nor do we assume lower interest rates, even though most economists (and the CBO) agree that balancing the budget would reduce them by at least one full percentage point. In this sense, our estimates are *extremely* conservative.

Despite our conservative approach, our carefully developed figures show a rapidly declining deficit and the emergence of a budget surplus by 2002. We are not foolish enough to maintain that these exact figures will materialize. But our spending cuts are all real and our conservative economic assumptions make it more likely that we will exceed than fall short of our targets. Barring a major economic downturn—always a possibility—a surplus in 2002 is an almost certain outcome if the People's Budget is enacted. And a surplus will permit the first reduction of the national debt since 1969.

Although our federal budget estimates do not take into account the impact of our proposals on the economy, it seems fair to point out that positive effects are very likely and that these effects would have very large and real benefits for the American people.

First, it is universally accepted that balancing the budget would spur economic growth. (If the budget is balanced, the federal government no longer has to borrow a larger portion of the nation's savings and more funds are available for private investment.) In testimony before the House Budget Committee early in 1995, Federal Reserve Board Chairman Alan Greenspan testified about the impact a balanced budget would have on Americans: "I think their real incomes and the purchasing power of their real incomes would significantly improve. . . . [T]hey would look forward to their children doing better than they are."

Indeed, if economic growth increased by one percentage point, on average, over seven years, each individual American would have $9,678 more income to spend over that period.

According to the Joint Economic Committee, the higher economic growth that a balanced budget would produce would also create over six million new jobs during the next ten years.

Others have estimated the impact of lower interest
rates—which economists believe would fall by at least one
percentage point—perhaps as much as two percentage
points—if the federal budget were balanced. Lower interest rates would reduce the cost of servicing the federal
debt. But more important, they would reduce the cost of
borrowing for all Americans. On a thirty-year, $75,000
home mortgage, for example, two percentage points trans-
lates into more than $37,000 in lower payments. Or, in
even more immediate terms, it would reduce payments on
a typical car loan by $180 a year.

CONCLUSION

The real payoff from the People's Budget is much
more profound than any set of economic statistics can capture. For at least twenty years, the American people have
been trying to recapture control of their government. Time
and time again they have sent their elected officials the
message that they want it smaller, leaner, less intrusive,
and, in what it is supposed to do, more effective.

The politicians in Washington have ignored each and
every message, stubbornly refusing to change their big-
spending, overregulating ways. Government has continued to grow, becoming more rather than less intrusive,
and more outmoded and inefficient with each passing
year. And the result has been a phenomenon even more
damaging than high taxes or a growing government debt:
The American people have begun to lose faith in their government and in their ability, as citizens, to change it. They
have begun to lose faith in the democratic process itself.
"Politics"—the word we use to define that process—has

become a dirty word.

The People's Budget is, therefore, more than a plan for cutting government spending, reducing taxes, or balancing the budget. It is a first, essential step on the road to restoring the trust of the American people in the most noble system of government ever conceived. For that reason, more than any other, we dearly hope that the emerging new majority, including members of both political parties, will hear the people's cries for change and find, in the People's Budget, a blueprint for bringing that change about. ★

APPENDIX ONE
Economic and Technical Assumptions

What about the economic assumptions behind our aggregate budget figures? Obviously, revenues turn crucially on the growth of the economy, and some outlays are affected by such things as the rate of inflation and the unemployment rate.

The American people are looking for one thing from Washington above all else: the truth. And certainly their budget should be based on an honest best-guess about what the economy is likely to do. Thus, we have resisted the temptation to turn to a "rosy scenario," an optimistic economic forecast, to make our totals look better. Moreover, *we have assumed no improvement in the economy as a result of our program, with its balanced budget and lower federal taxes.* We use the conservative CBO economic assumptions throughout. Their central element is modest average annual growth of the economy of 2.3 percent. Of course, the economy might do better than that with no federal deficit and lower taxes, but we do not make that assumption.

By the same token, we do not assume any impact of lower deficits on interest rates. The relationship between budget deficits and interest rates has long been a subject of debate among economists and financial market participants, and there are no clear answers. Interest rates appear to reflect primarily actual and expected inflation. Most people in this field, however, would expect that elimination of the current and prospective large deficit, as we propose, would result in lower interest rates than would otherwise prevail. This is because the total demand for borrowed funds would substantially decrease.

We have incorporated in our figures savings in outlays for interest on the debt, now approaching $250 billion a year and growing because of the slower growth and eventual small reduction of the national debt, as the deficits decline and turn into surpluses. This is standard practice. But we have not assumed any reduction of interest *rates*, even though lower rates are likely. In calculating outlays for interest, we have used the CBO interest rate forecast that is part of the economic assumptions noted above.

CBO itself, however, has made a calculation on the assumption that elimination of the deficit would bring down interest rates. If rates by the year 2000 were one full percentage point lower than currently assumed, the saving in that year in outlays for interest on the debt would be $38 billion. To repeat, we have *not* assumed such a savings in our budget.

We make one important and perhaps controversial

"technical" assumption. Specifically, we endorse and include in our totals the suggestion of Alan Greenspan, the chairman of the Federal Reserve Board, and of Robert Reischauer and June O'Neill, the former and current directors of the CBO, that the official Consumer Price Index (CPI) somewhat overstates inflation and that the annual cost-of-living increases in various programs should be adjusted accordingly.

The CPI is based on the buying patterns of a large sample of consumers in the early 1980s. If in that period a typical family bought eight pounds of steak in a week and twelve pounds of chicken, that is the "weight" given to steak and chicken in the index, and then subsequent price changes for each show up in the CPI. But what if steak goes up in price this year and chicken goes down? Obviously, families switch their buying and purchase more chicken and less steak. *So the actual cost of living to them has not gone up as much as the CPI indicates.*

This flaw is unavoidable in any price index. Ms. O'Neill testified to the Senate Finance Committee in early 1995, "A strong consensus exists that the CPI overstates the change in the cost of living by about 0.2 percentage points because it does not take into account how consumers respond to changing prices."

Other problems stem from the failure of the index to adjust for changes in quality. A perfect example is automobile tires. A standard tire in the base period cost, say, $60. Last month, as reported in the CPI, it cost $65, and the CPI goes up a little accordingly. But meanwhile, over the more than ten years since the base period, tire quality has improved so much that today's tire lasts for 50,000 miles compared with 25,000 miles in the early

1980s. The real cost of a tire has gone down, not up, but the CPI reports an increase.

Without going into further technicalities, suffice it to note that there is wide agreement among the experts that the CPI does overstate inflation. Mr. Greenspan, also testifying before the Senate Finance Committee, put the probable overstatement at between 0.5 percent and 1.5 percent. We have selected the conservative figure of 0.5 percent for our adjustment. That is, annual cost-of-living adjustments in various benefit programs—Social Security, federal civilian and military retirement, and a few others—would be computed by taking the CPI increase for the previous year minus one-half of 1 percent. The same adjustment would be made for the annual indexation of the income tax brackets, a change that would slightly increase revenues.

Our purpose, and that of Mr. Greenspan, is principally to make the annual Cost-of-living Adjustments in these programs more accurately reflect true inflation. There is no good reason to give retirees an increase every year that overcompensates them for the previous year's increase in prices. The change we propose does have a helpful effect on the budget, but not a huge one in a budget of $1.6 trillion. By the year 2000 adoption of the CPI-minus-0.5 formula would raise revenues by about $9.6 billion and reduce spending by about $13.3 billion. ★

APPENDIX TWO
Further Details on Major Proposals

This appendix provides further information about major proposals in the People's Budget:

Earned Income Tax Credit
Housing vouchers
Subsides to farmers and agribusiness
Medicare
Defense
Foreign Aid

EARNED INCOME TAX CREDIT

Before the EITC was enacted, the idea of an income supplement for the working poor had another name—the negative income tax. A fundamentally conservative idea, it was vigorously debated in the late 1960s and early 1970s and was the central concept behind President Richard Nixon's proposed "family assistance plan," which ultimately was rejected by Congress. The underlying and laudable purpose of the negative income tax was to make work more attractive than welfare and to add to the incomes of the unskilled and others who could not earn a "decent" wage.

But there was a big problem with the negative income tax. Obviously, it had to be phased down and then out as wage and salary income rose. This created a disincentive to more work and higher earnings; in effect there was a large extra "tax" (in the form of reduced negative income tax cash benefits) on each additional dollar earned. Several studies made at the time, based in part on pilot experiments, demonstrated the disincentive effect.

If, in an effort to solve this problem of a heavy tax on added earnings, the phaseout was made very gradual, two other problems raised their heads. The benefits and the incentives would be going to people with incomes far above the "working poor" level ($25,000 or even $30,000), and the cost of the program mounted to astronomical levels because benefits, though at a reduced level, would be going to a very large portion of the population. Congress found that it could not square this circle, which is the main reason it rejected the Nixon proposal. It was and remains impossible to accomplish all three aims simultaneously— an income supplement for the working poor phased out at higher incomes, little work disincentive, and reasonable cost.

The EITC was developed in the mid-1970s to solve what appeared to be a related and genuine problem. The federal income tax laws had gradually been changed so that working people with low wages paid little or no tax. But they paid full Social Security taxes of (now) 7.65 percent on their wages, no matter how low the wages. The goal of the EITC was to supplement the incomes of low-wage working families by roughly offsetting their Social Security taxes. Since 1990, however, the program has been liberalized so that for lower paid workers the EITC now does far more than offset the Social Security tax.

At very low earned incomes the EITC does what it is supposed to do—it actually subsidizes work effort. At incomes between $8,900 and $11,600 it slightly discourages work because recipients can work less and maintain the same income. But above $11,600—up to the limit of $28,500, where benefits cease altogether—the phaseout of benefits imposes a very real penalty on additional earnings. For a family with two children, the combination of the regular federal income tax bottom bracket rate of 15 percent, plus the Social Security tax, plus the EITC benefit reduction rate of 21 percent means that each additional dollar of earnings is "taxed" at a rate of 43.7 percent on incomes between $16,150 and $28,500. This is the same tax rate that is paid by taxpayers with incomes in excess of $140,000 a year!

The number of workers with very low wages whose work effort is subsidized by the EITC is far exceeded by those who are in the phaseout range of incomes where the disincentive comes into play. And, the higher the phaseout income range is extended in order to minimize the disincentive, the more millions of workers become eligible and the more the cost of the program skyrockets.

Marvin Kosters, a careful student of the EITC, has estimated that among married couples "about ten times as much output could be lost because of reduced work effort in the phaseout range [of incomes] as the output gained through increased work in the subsidy range." He acknowledges that these estimates are unavoidably imprecise, but the principal conclusion stands: "Incentives that have the effect of discouraging work and reducing output are large in relation to favorable work incentives under the EITC."

There is another problem with the EITC. *Given the way the EITC works, it pays workers at the low end of the earnings scale to overreport their earnings to the IRS in order to increase their benefits, and IRS has virtually no way to check on this it.* While there is no way of knowing how many people take advantage of the EITC in this way, many experts believe this sort of cheating is anything but rare.

As discussed earlier, we propose to replace the current EITC with a new and improved approach, which is actually a combination of two new tax credits.

The first would be a refundable tax credit of 7.65 percent of earned income (the amount of the Social Security tax) on the first $10,000 of earned income. This would apply to the earnings of all families with children, even the richest, but it would be refundable, of course, only for those earners with low incomes who owe no income tax. For those with higher incomes, as we shall note below, the revenue cost of this tax credit would be offset or "recaptured" by a small change in the income tax.

The second new credit would refund 10 percent of a family's earned income for each child up to four children, applied to the first $5,000 of earned income (meaning a maximum payment of $2,000 for a family with four or more children). Because it applies only to earned income, this subsidy would be available only to those who work.

If a family with two children earned $5,000, the two credits in combination would entitle it to a check from the federal government for $1,382. The combined credit for this family would rise to $1,765 at an income of $10,000, which provides a clear incentive to increase earnings. The maximum payment, to a family with four children earning $10,000, would be $2,765.

The new credit to offset Social Security taxes on the first $10,000 of earnings would accomplish the original purpose of the EITC, but would be costly in lost revenues. These can be largely recouped by reducing the income threshold at which the 15 percent income tax bracket kicks in by $5,100 for taxpayers with children. For a married couple with two children the 15 percent bracket would begin at an income of $11,050, versus $16,150 under current law. This change would increase the income tax slightly for taxpayers all the way up the income scale except for those whose earnings are very low and who thus pay little or no income tax. The higher income tax for most taxpayers would offset the credit they would get for Social Security taxes on the first $10,000 of earned income, leaving the after-tax income of taxpayers who pay taxes essentially unchanged. The tax structure as a whole would have been made more "progressive" because the employee payroll tax would be, in effect, abolished for the low-income workers.

HOUSING VOUCHERS

Housing vouchers are not a new idea. They were first used in the early 1970s, and today more than one million families and elderly individuals receive them and use them to obtain housing under several different programs.

Some of these programs have flaws, but the voucher principle itself has proved to be sound.

What is not sound are subsidies for the housing units themselves, which go either to local Public Housing Authorities (PHAs) or straight to developers. In both cases, the money is often wasted or used to perpetuate "projects" where conditions are hardly fit for human beings to live.

For example, John C. Weicher, a former assistant secretary at the Department of Housing and Urban Development, gave a good description of the problem with HUD's "modernization" programs—to rehabilitate rundown public housing—during congressional testimony early in 1995:

> Modernization sometimes seems to be a bottomless pit. Every few years there is a new study of modernization needs, and Congress raises the annual appropriation in response. Then a few years later there is another study, and it turns out that total modernization needs are higher than they were in the previous study, even after spending several billion dollars.

Under our proposal, PHAs would no longer receive grants from the government in Washington; instead, they would compete for tenants like every other apartment building—including tenants possessed of the new rental vouchers. Most existing tenants in the more decent projects probably would not move but would use their new vouchers to pay all or part of their rent.

Privately owned projects that now receive subsidies under contracts with HUD would not have their contracts renewed, but their tenants would receive vouchers that would allow them to continue renting in the same build-

ings. Private developers who have built low-income housing with a reasonable expectation of federal support and
who do a good job maintaining and operating their units
would thus continue to receive a subsidy—although now it
would come from the tenants. Forty percent of the residents in these projects are elderly, and in most cases the
residents are satisfied and the projects are well managed.
By continuing this support, albeit in a different form, we
propose that the federal government maintain its commitment to these elderly residents.

But government bailouts of privately owned apartment buildings that are badly managed would cease. If the
owner of the building threatened to go into default on his
federally insured mortgage, the default would be allowed
to occur, the government would take over the building and
sell it as soon as possible for the best price it could get—
rather than dumping more money into the hands of private developers who have shown they cannot get the job
done.

*In short, the government would get completely out of
the business of subsidizing buildings for low-income tenants. It would cease being banker, builder, or landlord.*
The United States has a record of nearly sixty years of failure when the government tries to do these things, with
huge waste of funds and all-too-frequent instances of
influence peddling and fraud. This can and should stop
right now.

The government's obligation to subsidize rents for
the approximately three million families who now receive
assistance under the various low-income housing programs would continue, though all of the families would get
their subsidy in the form of vouchers instead of only some

of them. All assisted families would choose their own
housing in the rental market, with the voucher helping
them to pay the rent.

Housing has never been an entitlement. Thus, while
the families presently subsidized should not be cut off,
there would be no further increase in the number of families receiving housing assistance, except for a small number now on the waiting lists equal to the number of vacant
units in public or private subsidized housing projects.

The budget savings from this change would come
principally in two ways. First, there would no longer be the
large outlays for building new public housing units and for
the aforementioned "modernization" of existing public
housing buildings ($3.5 billion was authorized in 1995
alone for this purpose) nor would any more money be
spent to rescue owners of privately owned subsidized
buildings faced with default on their mortgages. This
would be an early savings. Second, the extraordinary
growth in housing assistance spending as more families
are added to the rolls would cease, which would produce
increasing savings over time.

In addition to the various kinds of direct subsidies for
low-income housing there is also a special tax credit for
this purpose, which costs nearly $1.5 billion in revenues
this year and will cost more as time goes on. This credit,
while popular, is not very efficient. In a devastating cri-
tique of this program, the CBO reached these conclusions:

★ The low-income housing credit "is unlikely to increase
   substantially the supply of affordable housing" but rather
   "replaces other housing that would have been available
   through the private, subsidized housing market."

★ As compared to housing vouchers, the tax credit is an inefficient means of helping poor families. The tax credit "may allow investors to capture much of the benefits for themselves rather than their tenants" and "the housing that is subsidized through credits is more suited to the needs of investors than poor renters."

★ "The government can provide assistance of equal value to tenants through housing vouchers at a fraction of the cost of tax credits."

The low-income housing tax credit should be allowed to expire.

In 1970, only twenty-five years ago (and thirty-three years after the first federal public housing legislation was enacted during the New Deal) total federal spending on housing assistance was only $480 million. By 1980 it had climbed to $5.4 billion and by 1990 to $15.9 billion. In 1995 housing spending is estimated at $24.5 billion—fifty-one times the amount of twenty-five years ago and nearly four and one-half times as much as fifteen years ago. If all this money were producing clean, livable housing, that would be one thing. But to spend nearly $25 billion to be America's largest "slumlord" is simply wrong.

SUBSIDIES TO FARMERS AND AGRIBUSINESS

The array of farm programs is incredibly complex, even arcane. For the principal field crops like wheat and corn the main federal support program does two things. First, it ensures a floor under prices by accepting excess crops as collateral for government "loans" when the market price falls below the floor (if prices continue to be low, the farmer forfeits the crop and it goes into government stocks). Second, the government makes cash payments called "deficiency payments" to the farmers if market prices, while above the floor, are below a fictitious "target" price, fixed in law, designed to give the farmers a reasonable income. For other commodities the programs are different, and there are no direct subsidies at all for such major farm products as beef, pork, and poultry.

Overall, the array of farm programs breaks down into four main categories: commodity-specific subsidies, including "target" prices and deficiency payments; payments for placing farm acreage into "conservation" and "wetland" reserves and thus removing it from production; subsidized crop insurance, supplemented by "disaster" payments following droughts or floods or other blows from nature; and various kinds of export subsidies.

In the case of the commodity programs, the subsidies are not just federal outlays. For sugar, peanuts, and tobacco, the government holds up prices by limiting domestic production or controlling imports or both, ensuring good incomes for the producers of these crops with little or no federal spending. In these cases the subsidy is in effect provided by the consumer, who pays artificially high prices, rather than by the taxpayer. In the case of the complicated dairy program, the government seeks to hold up prices through anticompetitive "marketing orders" and then buys up any surpluses if prices threaten to decline despite the marketing orders.

Subsidies, therefore, cannot be measured by federal outlays alone. This became evident as the world's trading nations, acting through the General Agreement on Tariffs and Trade (GATT), sought to find a common denominator for measuring the agricultural subsidy practices of the different countries. This was a necessary component of the international negotiations aimed at reducing the barriers to trade in farm products.

As noted earlier, the GATT developed a reliable and reasonably accurate measure of the subsidies, so that one crop can be compared against another. This made it possible for the American public and Congress to know for the first time the true cost of the farm programs *to both taxpayers and consumers.*

In Chapter Four, we propose a "revenue insurance" approach to reforming farm subsidies. Another approach worth considering would directly tackle the inequity arising from the radically differing degrees of subsidy among the various farm products. Now that subsidies can be measured fairly, using the new GATT method, it is possible to reduce selectively the programs that have the highest ranked "subsidy equivalent" so that all farm commodities would receive roughly the same, fairly modest, degree of subsidization.

If the subsidy equivalent were fixed at 19 percent, applied to all the principal farm products, the savings by the late 1990s would be nearly $8 billion a year. The biggest losers, of course, would be the producers of the most heavily subsidized crops, such as rice.

MEDICARE

One impact of the Medicare proposals in the People's Budget will be to give people incentives to shift out of "fee-for-service" programs to coordinated care plans or Medical Savings Accounts. Because these alternatives are substantially more efficient, and thus less expensive, the budget savings from this shift are substantial.

We believe that the much lower cost to the Medicare beneficiary of coordinated care enrollment compared with fee-for-service programs will strongly encourage Medicare enrollment in these plans. Moreover, because these systems are being increasingly used by the younger population, more beneficiaries, as they approach retirement, will be in coordinated care plans and will be comfortable with them.

Currently, about 7 percent of beneficiaries each year are newly eligible. (Because about 5 percent die each year, the net growth in beneficiaries is under 2 percent.) Although it is impossible to know exactly how many Medicare beneficiaries will join coordinated care plans, we estimate that, by 2002, somewhere between 25 and 35 percent of total beneficiaries should be in the program.

It is perhaps surprising that those who officially estimate Medicare costs while preparing annual budgets may hesitate to assume that an increase in coordinated care participation will save money. This is a complex issue involving among other things the mix of relatively healthy beneficiaries in coordinated care plans versus fee-for-service plans, but these technical estimating issues need not concern us here. Significant increases in Medicare participation in HMOs and other coordinated care plans should reduce any problem that exists—but, ultimately, the issue must be decided with evidence, not theoretical arguments. Medicare can adjust its payments to coordinated care plans to offset any "adverse selection" (the case where healthier beneficiaries join coordinated care plans and those with more health problems stick with fee-for-service). Medicare should save money whether or not there is adverse selection.

In the short run, several reforms are both warranted and feasible.

First, post-acute care services (skilled nursing facilities, home health, and rehabilitation care) are the fastest growing part of Medicare. Between 1984 and 1994, these services grew from $2 billion to $16 billion, an annual increase of 35 percent. For the last ten years, hospitals have been paid for acute care services under the generally successful prospective payment system, based on the diagnosis of the patients' illness, not on the services they actually received. This has helped to control costs. Post-acute care services are not reimbursed in this manner, but they should be. Folding them into the prospective payment system would significantly reduce their growth rate. Hospitals would receive one payment, giving them an incentive to control the explosive growth in post-acute care.

Second, the great variation in the volume and intensity of physician services in hospitals should be addressed. Currently, such services account for about 35 percent of Medicare physician payments. After adjusting for differences in the illnesses of patients, about 25 percent of the nation's hospitals spend more than 120 percent of the national median. Payments to physician staffs that are extraordinarily high in volume of services per beneficiary can and should be reduced. This proposal would be the first since Medicare began that gives physicians a direct incentive to control volume and intensity.

A third proposal to control volume involves the payment made to hospitals for capital expenditures. Hospitals have average occupancy rates barely in excess of 60 percent. Yet, Medicare's payment for capital assumes that the hospital occupancy is 100 percent. We should pay hospitals based on their actual, not on their assumed, occupancy. Medicare should also make more use of competitive bidding for services, such as those for clinical labs.

Moreover, Medicare should create within the current system a preferred provider organization (PPO) for hospitals and physicians. In recent years, PPOs have become a major way to control growth of costs in private sector fee-for-service programs. Patients who use nonpreferred providers pay higher out-of-pocket amounts. In turn, preferred providers discount their payment rates and monitor the volume of services. Preferred providers who give excessive services are removed from the PPO. Medicare should adopt the method used in the private sector. Beneficiaries would have lower cost-sharing arrangements if they use a doctor or hospital on the list of preferred providers. Preferred providers would receive discounted fees.

We must also induce more cost-conscious behavior by beneficiaries. The original deductible for physician and related services has increased from only $50 to $100 during the entire history of the Medicare program, providing little incentive for beneficiaries to be cost conscious. Physician cost per enrollee has increased thirtyfold over the same period. On the other hand, the hospital deductible has risen steadily and is currently $716. To remedy the inequity between these deductibles and to bring cost sharing to relatively healthier (nonhospitalized) beneficiaries, the Part A (hospital) deductible should be decreased by $50 per year for four years while the Part B deductible would be increased by the same amount and then indexed by the increase of Part B program costs. Because beneficiaries use Part B for more episodes of care, this proposal would, on balance, increase beneficiary cost sharing and would reduce Medicare costs without imposing a significant burden on the Medicare population.

To save Medicare and prevent runaway growth, the system must also—perhaps unfortunately—continue the cost controls and cost sharing that already exist. The largest policy issue involves the Part B premium that beneficiaries pay, now $46.10 a month. Originally, the Part B premium was set up to pay 50 percent of the program's costs. Currently, the premium pays for only about 30 percent of Part B costs. To prevent the share of Medicare Part B costs covered by the premiums from dropping even further, the premium has been increased by about $5 per month in each of the last three years. Congress should continue the $5 increase in the years ahead. (Because the premium is deducted from Social Security checks and such checks increase annually with inflation, net beneficiary checks would still increase.)

It might be objected that because most Medicare beneficiaries have Medigap policies that pay most, if not all, out-of-pocket costs, these increases in cost sharing will have no impact on beneficiary incentives. This objection is faulty. Increases in required cost sharing will, at a minimum, require an increase in Medigap policy premiums. Moreover, the current Medigap rules should be changed to allow—but not require—cheaper no-frills Medigap policies, in which beneficiaries would have only major out-of-pocket expenses covered. At least some beneficiaries would shift toward no-frills plans.

Another policy that should be continued involves the annual update of payments made to hospitals under the prospective payment system. Congress determines this update, which is supposedly based on several variables, including input inflation (called the "market basket"), hospital practice patterns, and hospital productivity. Over the next four years Congress should continue the recent policy of setting the update at well below the market basket. After the next four years, a productivity factor should be incorporated in the annual hospital update. The assumption in the present system is that Congress will set the annual update amount at the full value of the market basket, ignoring the other variables. Congress in most years has set the update at about one-half of the market basket, and this should continue.

Many hospitals argue that this annual update system underpays them, because Congress allows less than a full inflation adjustment for higher wages and the like. This claim is incorrect. First of all, the market basket ignores productivity improvements. As in most aspects of American business, hospitals improve their productivity. Even ignoring productivity, the actual increase in payments by Medicare per case greatly exceeds not only the actual update enacted by Congress but also the market basket. How could this be? The reason is a phenomenon call "creep," which means that hospitals continually classify illnesses and the resulting payments into categories for which they receive higher reimbursement.

Further, it is worth noting that unlike most other payers, Medicare pays hospitals additional amounts above the basic prospective payment system payment, including payments for capital, for bad debts, for teaching hospitals, and for hospitals with unusually high proportions of poor patients. These additional payments can and should be reformed.

In the mid-1980s, Medicare established an additional payment for hospitals with a disproportionate share (DSH) of low-income patients. The same principle was adopted for the companion Medicaid program, which provides medical care for the poor. Soon many states found a loophole in Medicaid rules for DSH payments that allowed them to juggle payments to and from hospitals in such a way as to make the federal government pay the full cost of Medicaid instead of slightly more than half as the program intended. This has been a huge cost to the federal taxpayer. Our proposal would reduce the Medicare DSH payment to hospitals by the increases in federal Medicaid outlays resulting from the loophole in the Medicaid rules.

Another significant change in hospital payments involves the so-called indirect teaching adjustment for teaching hospitals, which is currently 7.7 percent for each 0.1 percent increase in the ratio of teaching residents to beds. This adjustment is provided to cover the higher cost that teaching hospitals believe they incur in treating Medicare patients. Many studies show that this adjustment overcompensates teaching hospitals, and most of the 1994 health care reform bills contained provisions reducing it. We follow those suggestions and propose a reduction to 3 percent.

These interim reforms would slow the cost growth of Medicare. In the longer run, increased use of coordinated care would produce even more substantial savings, though Medicare would continue to grow.

REFORMING THE PENTAGON
Management Changes

The change in Clinton administration priorities in favor of increased national and international social spending by the federal government has had a negative impact on the ability of the defense establishment to respond to national defense needs appropriate to the twenty-first-century security environment. To mitigate the effect of unfavorable policy and resource allocation choices over the past several years, an aggressive program of management change is needed.

Changes in the Centralized Management of DOD and service functions

The demobilization of more than one-third of the Cold War-era defense establishment since the Gulf War has not been accompanied by changes to centralized DOD and service resources. While there has been a massive reduction in procurement from the private sector (a two-thirds decline since the mid-1980s), DOD and service depots and laboratories, development, and testing activities have not been proportionately affected. The severe meltdown in procurement from the private sector has adversely affected the ability of the defense industrial base to respond to military contingencies and has significantly diminished the diversity of the base as a result of the DOD-encouraged consolidation of the industry into a few large organizations. This trend can be mitigated through the privatization of the DOD and service depot and laboratory structure.

By transferring development and support functions now undertaken by DOD and service elements to the private sector, the need for a DOD subsidy to "military unique" technology will no longer be required, and the private sector defense industrial base will be able to maintain a broader residual capacity to meet future requirements.

The Clinton administration has been reluctant to extend the base realignment and closure (BRAC) activities as aggressively as required. As a consequence, the DOD budget continues to carry the burden of unneeded facilities. Moving forward with both BRAC and depot and development sector privatization in parallel can produce significant savings over the Five-Year Defense Program (FYDP).

DOD military personnel practices also provide a fruitful arena for savings. The number of new accessions annually accounts for nearly one-third of the active duty force. This figure drives the size and cost of the training base, and the duration of their service impacts the cost of the military retirement system. The cost of the military personnel system can be reduced compared with the present circumstances by increasing the length of the initial enlistment, while providing disincentives for most new accessions so they do not seek a career of sufficient length to render them eligible for the military retirement system. FYDP savings = $13.5 billion.

Financial management

DOD is virtually alone among large-scale economic entities in financing its asset procurement by maximizing front-end costs. By paying virtually the full cost of acquisition of assets with an economic life of a quarter century or more, it minimizes the flexibility of current Budget Authority, (appropriations) rather than matching more closely the cost of acquisition to the economic life of the asset.

Two reforms can be implemented that can significantly diminish the expenditure of near-term BA for critical acquisition efforts. The first involves the increased use of incremental rather than full funding for major asset acquisitions. Incremental funding is already widely used in the procurement of B&D services and for selected intelligence collection and processing platforms. The use of "long lead" procurement, especially for shipbuilding, has moved toward incremental funding but has not achieved the full benefits incremental funding offers. Low production rate (and acquisition objectives) of major platforms makes it desirable that production lines be extended despite the impact of such an approach on unit costs. In the case of the production of highly specialized platforms such as major naval combatants and heavy bomber aircraft, incremental funding can spread the cost of acquisition over its period of manufacture. The period of manufacture in turn can be manipulated if necessary to accommodate circumstances that require either an acceleration or a slow down in the rate of production.

Second, the DOD has relied more than is desirable on government sources of finance for its modernization. There are substantial opportunities to privatize the finance of elements of defense procurement through the use of commercial financing practice. For example, the use of lease finance permits a better match between the cost of acquisition and its useful life than a conventional procurement using public sector finance. The near- and medium-term emphasis on the use of commercial products and/or specifications and subsystem upgrades to existing platforms provides a constructive opportunity to extend the domain of privatized financing to defense procurement.

FYDP saving = $15 billion.

Procurement reform

The public accounting firm, Coopers and Lybrand,

recently published a review of the cost of DOD procurement regulation, *The DOD Regulatory Cost Premium: A Quantitative Assessment.* The results of this study are consistent with several other studies (e.g., National Performance Review, the Carnegie Commission, and the Defense Science Board) on the effect of DOD procurement regulation on contractor costs. The study concludes that procurement regulations increase the cost of procurement to the contractor (and ultimately to DOD and the taxpayer) by 18 percent.

Despite a decade of pseudo reform, little has been accomplished. The 103rd Congress missed the most recent opportunity to exact fundamental reform despite Secretary of Defense Perry's constructive effort to facilitate the integration of commercial products and practices into DOD procurement. Instead, only a modest advance was made under the guise of procurement "streamlining." The Coopers and Lybrand study identifies the specific regulatory problems with sufficient clarity to provide an unambiguous guide to regulatory change and/or statutory revision to permit capturing a large fraction of the considerable savings available from implementation of such a reform. One of the useful lessons of research, development, test, and evaluation (RDT&E) and procurement during the 1980s, when the role of classified programs in the DOD grew significantly, is the beneficial effect on cost and schedule of the diminished cadre of auditors, inspectors, and program reviewers that normally impose high costs on conventional procurements.

Secretary Perry's initiative to increase the role of commercial products and practices has not been followed up by accompanying changes in the federal acquisition regula-

tions. As a consequence, bewildered DOD contracting offi-
cers find themselves lacking the regulatory authority to
implement what they otherwise understand to be public
policy. Statutory implementation of a broad grant of waiver authority to senior officials will enable the introduction
of commercial products and practices to accelerate.
The success of such an initiative assumes greater
importance in the years ahead as the technologies of
information warfare spell the difference between the timely modernization of U.S. forces and their probable defeat
by another nation that is more aggressive about the adap-
tion of "commercial" information-age technology to military purposes. No technology since the application of
atomic energy to military purposes has such potential for
revolutionary change.

FYDP savings: $10 billion.

POLICY CHANGE

The policy change with the greatest potential for savings is to terminate the current requirment that the DOD
fund programs unrelated to DOD missions. The FY1995
level of such funding is $11 billion (not including $5 billion
in environmental costs). The administration's domestic
spending agenda could not be accommodated within
existing budget caps, so the funds were expended via the
DOD. These unwise diversions should be ended.

FYDP savings = $50 billion.

RESOURCE ALLOCATION IN THE CLINTON
ADMINISTRATION—NEAR-TERM READINESS

The Clinton administration assumed control of the
executive branch in 1993 with an extensive agenda for the

increased involvement of the federal government in the civil sector of American life, including the domestic economy, education, welfare, medical care, housing, civil works infrastructure, and so on. Its domestic agenda was to be financed by an increase in taxation, containing the outyear cost of the federal medical care system, and reductions in defense expenditure. To distance itself from the Bush administration's "base force" concept (which established a post-Cold War force structure baseline), the Clinton administration initiated a "Bottom Up Review" (BUR) designed to narrow the focus of post-Cold War defense objectives so that defense expenditures could fit into the diminished aggregate amount of resources anticipated for the national defense function.

From the outset, the BUR force structure was underfunded. The force structure required to sustain a post-Cold War contingency assumption of two near-simultaneous major regional contingencies, such as Desert Storm, could not be financed within the budget constraints driven by the administration's demanding domestic and international social agenda. The General Accounting Office (GAO) estimate of the extent of current BUR underfunding is $150 billion. This figure somewhat overstates the magnitude of the problem in the near term, but the trend identified by the GAO is clear. Further political constraints were imposed within the defense budget that have significantly degraded both short- and long-term readiness to cope with military contingencies.

Mindful of the travail of the Carter administration in coping with charges of a lack of "readiness," the administration has focused its resource allocation to avoid such criticism. It has done so by funding the best-known measures of current readiness (e.g., U.S. Navy steaming days per quarter and U.S. Navy/U.S. Air Force flying hours per crew/month) and "quality of life" enhancements, while underfunding other dimensions of short-term readiness.

The shift in the administration's foreign policy emphasis from traditional alliance (bilateral/multilateral) structures to dependence on the United Nations has led to a sustained high level of military operations (OPTEMPO). FY 1995 O&M expenditure increased 6 percent over the prior year despite a 2.5 percent reduction in military end strength. This increase reflected the significantly higher OPTEMPO of deployed forces in coping with the (largely unreimbursed) demands of the United Nations operations in forty countries. The increased levels of sustained military operations has caused a rapid increase in maintenance backlogs. Unfunded depot maintenance has increased from $500 million in FY 1992 to four times that number in FY 1995. The unfunded backlog of maintenance and repairs has more than tripled from the average level in the 1980s to nearly $15 billion. Similarly, unfunded real property maintenance backlogs for the armed services have increased to more than $13 billion from an average level of one-third that figure during the 1980s. As a metaphor for the problem of the neglect of core short-term readiness, the last Marine Corps amphibious vehicle to be withdrawn from Somalia suffered an engine breakdown as it was defending Somalia, resulting from deferred maintenance. It had to be towed through the surf to its amphibious assault ship.

RESOURCE ALLOCATION IN THE CLINTON ADMINISTRATION—LONG-TERM READINESS

While the responsiveness of the defense establishment for near-term contingencies affecting American security interests has been diminished by resource allocation practices under the Clinton administration, the most severe damage has been done to the readiness function in the long term. Long-term readiness is determined by near-term expenditure in the investment accounts; RDT&E and procurement. Defense equipment, particularly weapon platforms such as naval combatants, aircraft, and armored vehicles are long-lived and costly assets. These must be designed in a manner appropriate to the conduct of military operations for decades ahead and procured in sufficient numbers to provide for the desired military effect.

Unfortunately, the investment accounts have served as the "bank" within the DOD to finance sustaining levels

DOD PROCUREMENT
FY85–FY95
(billions, FY95 $)

FY85	132.7	FY91	80.2
FY86	122.8	FY92	68.5
FY87	102.8	FY93	55.9
FY88	98.8	FY94	45.8
FY89	94.5	FY95	43.3
FY90	93.7		

Total reduction FY85–95 $89.4 billion

of operating and military personnel expenditure. While
funding for the operating accounts has been stabilized, the
procurement account funding has been drastically cur-
tained. Measured in FY 1995 dollars, procurement expenditure has declined from $132 billion in FY 1985 to $43 billion in FY 1995.

A two-thirds reduction in procurement expenditure
has had a number of important consequences. The U.S.
Air Force has ceased procuring new combat aircraft; no
new combat aircraft will be procured in either FY 1995 or
FY 1996 for the first time since the 1930s. The U.S. Army
has ceased procuring new tanks; only upgrades to existing
vehicles are being performed. U.S. Navy shipbuilding has
declined by 80 percent from more than twenty ships per
year in the 1980s.

To cope with the steep decline in procurement, the
truncated force structure (reduced by 32 percent since FY
1987) has been equipped with the most modern platforms
in the inventory in FY 1994. The impact of such a set of
decisions is predictable; the simultaneous aging of the
inventory of military platforms. These platforms are
approaching the mid-point in their operational life. In the
absence of a change in policy, a president in the first
decade of the twenty-first century will face the problem of
the virtual en bloc obsolescence of the core of American
military power. Financing the recovery of such a broadly
based pattern of obsolescence will require a very intense
and costly buildup. The replacement value of DOD's asset
base is $2.6 trillion. Given a nominal useful life of a mod-
ern military platform of twenty-five years, annual depreciation on the asset base is $100 billion.

Yet procurement expenditures (under the Clinton

HISTORICAL DOD & MILITARY DEPARTMENT

Procurement/RDT&E Ratio FY 59-FY 95 *(in billions)*	
Procurement	$3.2
RDT&E	1.2
Total	$4.4
Procurement to RDT&E Ratio (DoD)	2.6:1
Procurement to RDT&E (Army)	2.5:1
Procurement to RDT&E (Navy)	3.9:1
Procurement to RDT&E (Air Force)	2.4:1

administration defense program) will not resume a positive rate of growth until 1997 from a base of only $39 billion in FY 1996. The historical relationship between procurement and RDT&E has been in a ratio of 2.6:1 since the mid-1950s.

By FY 1996, this ratio has fallen to virtually 1:1, and when disguised reductions in military RDT&E are eliminated (i.e., expenditures unrelated to DOD's mission such as breast cancer research, support for the Olympics, etc.) the ratio is less than one-to-one. The result is a pattern of resource allocation that will not support the readiness and sustainability of U.S. armed forces in the coming decade.

FY 1996–2001 National Defense Budget
Force structure augmentation

A modest increase in U.S. Army force structure from the existing fifteen plus division equivalents to sixteen divisions is needed. This increase assumes the ability of the Army to reclaim a significant portion of the 85,000 troops currently detached to other duties (e.g., U.N. ser-

vice). The Marine Corps force structure should be augmented by a brigade-equivalent (3,000 troops). The Navy
force structure should be increased by thirty-five major
combatants over FY 1995 levels (to 400 ships including an
additional aircraft carrier). One additional U.S. Air Force
air wing (from the FY 1995 level of twenty) should be
added.

   To restrain O&M growth, OPTEMPO can be reduced
by diminishing the United Nations' on unreimbursed use
of DOD resources. In addition, the use of sequenced
readiness procedures will diminish the tendency to over-
invest in near-term readiness at the expense of long-term
readiness, i.e., modernization via the investment accounts.
Intelligence collection and processing has been under-
mined by budget reductions. The shift in focus from a
specified geographic area and political culture (i.e., the
former Soviet bloc) to a disparate collection of worldwide
threats imposes new demands on the intelligence community for which the nature of the Soviet threat left it largely
unprepared.

RDT&E augmentation

   Despite the best intentions of the current DOD leadership to sustain investment in the RDT&E accounts, the
combined impact of the administration's domestic social
welfare agenda, its appetite for nondefense-related expenditure within the DOD budget, and the unreimbursed costs
for DOD support of multilateral agencies such as the United Nations have conspired to encumber these intentions.
The rapid advances in civil technology, particularly related to information warfare, are not being exploited with the
rapidity justified by the payoff to be gained in military

effectiveness. RDT&E needs to be augmented by 20 percent over FY 1995 levels over the course of the FYDP. This reverses the administration's policy of RDT&E disinvestment, which has proposed more than a 20 percent RDT&E reduction over the FYDP.

Procurement augmentation

As noted, over the past four decades, procurement expenditure has averaged 2.6 times that of RDT&E in the DOD. Successful introduction of commercial technology and practices and other policy changes will mitigate the need to regain this historic ratio. Nevertheless, the procurement account has to be increased to take advantage of the benefits of modern technology to support national security policy objectives. Among the significant programmatic initiatives are the following:

★ Initiate development and procurement of the U.S. Navy's "upper tier" missile defense system to augment existing TMD programs and provide a first-generation missile defense capability to U.S. forward deployed forces, as well as provide protection to U.S. civilians against missile attack

★ Restore advanced aircraft procurement funds including near-term F-22 funding and resumption of F-15 and F-16 procurements

★ Resume procurement of advanced low-observable aircraft procurement, including a B-2 restart and a naval variant of the F-117 via incremental funding

★ Enhance strategic/theater mobility, including restoration of the C-17 acquisition objective to 120 platforms and acceleration of the introduction of the C-130J

★ Accelerate tri-service information warfare and digitization procurements
★ Introduce precision surveillance/targeting/strike platforms and munitions
★ A modest BA growth over the FY 1995 base is needed to address shortfalls in core capabilities created by the Clinton administration's diversion of defense resources to nondefense purposes. Despite this modest augmentation of BA (1.5 percent per annum over the last three years of the FYDP), the aggregate amount allocated to the national defense function is below the growth path established under the Bush administration's "base force" concept.

DETAILS ON FOREIGN ASSISTANCE REDUCTIONS

International Development and Humanitarian Assistance (Budget Function 151)

Budget Function 151 accounts for 43 percent of the expenditures in the entire international affairs budget function, and it is the sector that has made the fewest adjustments to changes in the international environment. This account contributes little to achieving American foreign policy objectives. The goals of the program, though a somewhat confused muddle as a result of more than three decades of political fashion du jour reflected in the underlying legislative authority (the Foreign Assistance Act of 1961, as amended), are directed at broad economic development and humanitarian objectives. Results in the low-income countries have been doubious at best. From the perspective of budget priorities, investment in this account is disproportionate to American policy interests, and considerable savings can be made here.

De-emphasize multilateral development expenditures

While the capability of international financial institutions—chiefly, the International Monetary Fund—to respond to temporary international monetary instability is a potentially useful option for American foreign policy, the case for multilateral economic development assistance is notably less sound. While proponents argue on behalf of international development spending by multilateral institutions on the basis of the leverage these institutions provide for "modest" U.S. investment, the prior question is the efficacy of such expenditures. Whether development assistance is provided on a multilateral or bilateral basis, it has little behavioral impact on the recipient. In the case of multilateral expenditure, there is considerable reticence in denying funding to institutions that retard development by reinforcing state intervention in the economy.

An extreme example of the problem is reflected in the aid experience in the Newly Independent States (NIS) of the former Soviet Union. It has recently been reported in a study by the Bank for International Settlements that in the case of Russia, for example, capital outflows have virtually equalled post-Communist capital inflows. These capital inflows, both multilateral and bilateral have, in too many cases, simply reinforced the dominance of state institutions over economic initiative and resource allocation. Through the end of 1993, the international community has disbursed $23 billion to the NIS. The impact of the transfers has largely been counterproductive.

**Restructure bilateral development assistance to limit
its use to technical assistance**

Nearly 15 percent of the international development
account supports the bilateral Sustainable Development
Assistance Program. This, coupled with a separate but
related Development Fund for Africa and a number of
smaller AID programs, is the core of the government's
development assistance activities abroad. While the ailments of the program have been widely exposed, little
ingenuity apart from rhetorical flourish has been invested
in the program for many years. Despite the wish of successive administrations to alter the program, an effective
lobby of 42,000 personnel supported by the program have
frustrated the reform process. The contribution to policy
change in recipient countries is so small some nations
have received aid for five decades.

The residual function of the development assistance
program should be narrowly limited to the provision of
technical advisory services directly associated with the
transition to market-oriented reform. Assistance with
such functions as the creation of the legal and regulatory
environment to establish a market system, creation of a
modern financial sector, and similar services can provide
a smoother path to development, particularly when coupled with a liberalized trading environment. Such an
approach will not eliminate development assistance as an
element of the foreign assistance program but will reduce
its cost substantially and refocus its application to its most
useful function. Peripheral organizations such as the
Peace Corps are significant resource consumers ($234
million in FY 1996 BA) but contribute little to the market-
oriented transformation of developing nations.

The reform process in the former Communist states of Europe has been handicapped by the reluctance of both Europe and, to a lesser extent, the United States to permit access to their markets. Experience from the post-World War II period with the devastated economies of Europe and Asia revealed that access to international hard currency markets was a crucial element in their recovery. The economies of the NIS and Central and Eastern Europe have not suffered the physical destruction that stimulated the Marshall Plan in the late 1940s. Only policy reform and trade access, not insufficient aid flows, prevents the emergence of the former Communist states of Europe as economically successful democracies.

International Security Assistance
(Budget Function 152)

From the perspective of achieving U.S. foreign policy objective abroad, the security assistance function is the highest leverage account of the international affairs activities of the U.S. government. It is a crucial instrument of U.S. foreign policy in part because the U.S. government has a virtual worldwide monopoly on comprehensive security assistance services. Ironically, it has been the account that has been cut most deeply since the mid-1980s.

The reasons for the efficiency of security assistance expenditures are not obscure. As a consequence of national investment in cutting-edge military capabilities and a military strategy that emphasizes forward deployment and an expeditionary military posture, the United States is able to offer the world's most cost-effective array of weapons systems, training, maintenance, and other support services. Moreover, because American defense products are periodically updated to accommodate to changes in the military threat, foreign users receive de facto access to the U.S. intelligence system.

The employment of the security assistance instrument, either through cash arms sales or financed through the Foreign Military Financing (FMF) mechanism, has permitted the president to assume the lead in circumstances as diverse as repelling Iraq's invasion of Kuwait through a thirty-two-nation multinational coalition and acting on North Korea's efforts to acquire weapons of mass destruction. While the end of the Cold War fueled optimism that security-related concerns would diminish in bilateral as well as regional affairs, the opposite has emerged. Local and regional tension poses a powerful short- as well as long-term threat to the enduring American interest: to create and sustain an environment in which political pluralism and economic dynamism can exist.

The largest account in the International Security Assistance budget is the FMF account. The account is dominated by grants of $1.8 billion to Israel and $1.2 billion to Egypt. This expenditure has played an important historic role in the Middle East peace process and has been a central feature of Egypt's movement to establish ties with the West. To this end, it has enabled Egypt, as the largest Arab state, to moderate the influence of radical Islam in the Arab world. Israel's highly modern military establishment continues to play an important regional security role in containing the influence of the radical states in the region including Iran, Iraq, Syria, and Libya.

By moving toward an integrated approach to the financing of the security assistance function, the utility of the effort to the president can be significantly increased while the budgetary cost of doing so can be reduced from present levels. This result can be achieved by the creation of a defense export loan guarantee program, that does not include provisions for a credit subsidy. This account can be employed when the president decides an arms transfer will advance American foreign policy interest (i.e., is consistent with the Arms Export Control Act), but the buyer's cash flow profile makes a cash procurement infeasible. The loan guarantee program would, for example, provide the president with notably more flexibility than he now has to address U.S. needs to accelerate the conversion of the former Communist states of Central Europe to an ability to interoperate with NATO. In general, the program would enable the president to shift creditworthy FMF grant recipients to an account that requires little budget outlay.

In circumstances where it was desirable to provide concessional credit assistance to allied nations, a grant account could be employed to "buy down" the effective rate of interest on the credit provided through the loan guarantee program. A residual grant element can be retained to provide FMF grant assistance for non-creditworthy recipients when it is in the national interest to do so.

Conduct of Foreign Affairs
(Budget Function 153)

The centralization of the major international affairs functions in the Department of State through its absorption of AID, ACDA, and USIA will significantly increase the department's operating costs, but this will be more than offset by savings provided by the disestablishment of these agencies. The absorption of AID, ACDA, and the USIA make structural reform of the Department of State unavoidable. Reforming State's management superstructure into a tighter and more coherent entity to manage its policy and resource base can produce substantial savings. These savings can be redeployed in part to strengthen the department's traditional diplomatic functions and finance the transition costs associated with the process of centralizing the international affairs functions in the Department of State.

If the Congress elects to abolish the Department of Commerce (DOC), it is possible that further consolidation of some of the DOC functions such as export control and the management of the Foreign Commercial Service might be absorbed by the Department of State. The impact of these changes would be profound and would require fundamental reforms in the management of the department in Washington as well as at diplomatic missions abroad.

Foreign Information and Exchange Activities (Budget Function 154)

Information and exchange activities serve an important purpose in the implementation of U.S. foreign policy objectives. However, the infrastructure for doing so is vastly in excess of contemporary requirements. Moreover, the independence of USIA from the Department of State has caused some of its programs to become decoupled from their central purpose—advancing specific U.S. foreign policy interests. Each of the programmatic thrusts of USIA can be constructively reformed and their costs substantially diminished while strengthening the Department of State's public diplomacy.

Foreign information activities

Both State and USIA maintain parallel information-related activities, although USIA's is notably larger. Centralizing and rationalizing these information activities can sharply reduce the cost of foreign information activities.

International broadcasting operations

USIA has been slow to engage new technologies that would provide more effective means of communication to advance the public diplomacy function. While shortwave radio will be a channel of continuing importance in developing nations and in those where access to information is denied, commercial interests have long relied on other technologies for the transmission of information. Exploitation of the rich private telecommunications infrastructure can provide a more efficient means of reaching target audiences than the costly (one-third of the USIA's BA) reliance on the existing international broadcast infrastructure. Moreover, the end of the Cold War has created substantial excess capacity in the shortwave broadcasting sector that can mitigate the demand for system mode

International educational and cultural exchanges

These activities have in many cases become detached from the needs of U.S. diplomacy. This is so despite the fact that educational and cultural exchanges can serve useful policy ends. Rationalizing these programs by the Department of State to respond more directly to U.S. policy interests will permit this often helpful medium-term instrument of policy to support overall foreign policy objectives.

International Financial Programs
(Budget Function 155)

This account primarily reflects the cost of loan subsidies for the Export-Import Bank. The cost of these activities could be substantially reduced if the credit subsidy were reduced or phased out in a manner parallel to the approach discussed for the special case of defense exports. The primary driver in official export credit support is the availability of credit rather than its cost. Elimination of the subsidy would not prevent credit from being made available to creditworthy nations. For those nations where a foreign policy interest was served by offering an export credit subsidy, provisions can be made for doing so. This requirement is unlikely to justify the high level of subsidies contained in the program for FY 1996.

There is a separate but equally limited justification for the budgeting for credit subsidies—these serve as an instrument for dissuading other nations from using large-scale subsidies for the financing of specific export transactions. The "war chest" concept has been used episodically in the past. The demand for such a program is likely to be modest in view of the increasing difficulties many nations are encountering in their efforts to subsidize the cost of finance to selected foreign buyers of their products.

Foreign Affairs Budget Recommendations

De-emphasis on multilateral assistance and international organizations

A $700 million (36 percent) reduction in support for multilateral development banks and international organizations can be accomplished while leaving sufficient resources to carry out useful multilateral functions.

Bilateral development assistance

The abolition of AID, and a refocusing of aid to initiatives that impact the ability of the president to implement foreign policy objectives abroad allows significant economies to be obtained. The reduction in AID programs, particularly in Sustainable Development Assistance, permits a reduction in the personnel carried over to the Department of State. Bilateral assistance to the states of the former Soviet Union has slowed policy reform and should be reduced and limited to technical assistance directly related to policy reform.

International Security Assistance

The high-leverage security assistance account can offer improved responsiveness to national needs at lower costs through the shift to the use of loan guarantees and diminished dependence on grant assistance. The use of loan guarantees without a credit subsidy derived from appropriated funds will enable the president to facilitate access to the U.S. defense market for creditworthy nations and facilitate achieving the objectives of the Arms Export Control Act. Transformation of the Middle East region security assistance activity can be initiated by converting a portion of Israel's current grant assistance to a loan guarantee form (parallel to the pre-FY 1985 structure). Such an approach will permit the Israeli Ministry of Defense to finance its modernization to cope with the proliferation of threats from non-contiguous states in the region more effectively than it can with the declining (in real terms) grant FMF allocation they have received since FY 1985.

Miscellaneous foreign operations programs

A shift in emphasis in bilateral assistance from resource transfer to technical assistance eliminates the need for the Peace Corps. The low level of effectiveness of the International Narcotics Program suggests the need to begin to shift resources from this account to more effective anti-crime measures. The Export-Import Bank should initiate a transformation of its activities away from its current credit-subsidized basis to the use of unsubsidized transactions similar to the approach proposed to support the International Security Assistance program. ★

APPENDIX THREE
Additional Spending Cuts

This appendix presents illustrative examples of program reforms, reductions, and terminations not listed in the text.

Account	Policy	Policy Rationale	1995	Proposed Funding	Savings
DEPARTMENT OF AGRICULTURE					
Rural Water & Waste Disposal Grants	Terminate	This is a local responsibility. Localities have decreased their contribution as they have received federal funds.	500	0	500
Rural Bus. Enterprise Grants	Terminate	Rural economic development projects are local responsibility.	47.5	0	47.5
Rural Develop. Loan Fund	Terminate	Rural economic development projects are local responsibility.	47.5	0	47.5
Foreign Agricultural Service	Terminate	This is a subsidy to exporters.	108.9	0	108.9
Agricultural Marketing Service	Terminate marketing functions. Inspections and standardization functions to be funded through offsetting collections.	Agribusiness needs no help marketing; marketing services should be privately funded.	56	0	56
Agricultural Conservation Prgm.	Terminate	Soil & Water Conservation programs are already housed in the NRCS & EPA, and similar projects are also run by the Bureau or Reclamation and Corp. of Engineers. Proliferation of programs leads to duplication and support for low priority programs.	100	0	100

Account	Policy	Policy Rationale	1995	Proposed Funding	Savings
Econ. Research Service National Agricultural Statistics		Combine two departments and privatize commodity market data collection and dissemination.	134.3	67	67
Agricultural Research Svc. *(Includes Building & Facilities Account)*		Bureau should focus on basic research that is unlikely to be done by the private sector. Research facilities should be consolidated.	758.3	379.15	379.15
Extension Service		Eliminate programs that are duplicative of Research & Education Activities, or are not farming related, i.e. Youth at Risk & Nutrition Education Initiative.	136.8	0	136.8
Agric'l. Credit Insurance Fund		Farmers, like all others, should pay market rates for loans.	161	0	161
Emergency Food Assistance	Terminate	The program was intended to be temporary. It has served its purpose, so it should be terminated.	65	0	65
Land Acquisition Accounts	Terminate	Govt. owns enough land. Mgmt. of existing inventory shifted to operating account.	65.2	0	65.2
State & Private Forestry	Terminate Coop. Forestry programs.	This is a grab bag of state jobs, research and environmental programs, which should be funded by state and local entities.	161.3	48.7	112.6
Forest Research	Cut to 1988 inflation adjusted level.	This account is one of the many accounts which have increased rapidly, with an emphasis on environmental concerns, while ignoring the benefits and costs of the regulations.	200.1	177.5	22.6

Account	Policy	Policy Rationale	1995	Proposed Funding	Savings
National Forest System		Return to pre 1990 total forest & timber harvest level. This will significantly increase offsetting collections. These funds will be used to decrease the deficit, and not to reduce appropriations, hence no large reduction is shown here.	1345	1277.75	67.25
Construction	Terminate Funds for road const.	These funds provide access to low priced timber for timber purchasers.	203.2	103.2	100

DEPARTMENT OF COMMERCE
This Dep't. will be merged with the Dep't. of Labor and will be called Dep't. of Commerce & Labor.

Account	Policy	Policy Rationale	1995	Proposed Funding	Savings
Economic Dev. Admin.		This agency and its programs serve narrow & specialized local and regional political interests. Decisions as to local development projects should be determined & paid for by local entities, private or governmental.	440	0	446
Minority Bus. Dev. Agency		Eliminate set-asides and race-based policies. Remaining funds combined with SBA advocacy funds for advocacy purposes.	43.9	2.7	41.2
U.S. Travel & Tourism Admin.	Terminate	This agency funds promotional activities whose benefits accrue to private travel-related industries.	16.4	0	16.4
Technology Admin. Office of Technology Policy	Terminate	This agency supports industrial policy research, which, given the Federal			

Account	Policy	Policy Rationale	1995	Proposed Funding	Savings
		government's track-record, should be done by the private sector.	10	0	10
Nat'l. Telecomm. & Info. Admin		We have multiple communications agencies & we do not need this one. Bureau's essential duties, i.e. spectrum management, should be transferred to the FCC. The majority of the remaining funds are for "information infrastructure grants"; the creation of "information infrastructure" is best performed by private industry.	116.5	12	104.5
Nat'l. Inst. of Standards & Technology		Terminate Industrial Policy Act, which supports the formation of U.S. "industrial policy & competitiveness," a task best left to the market. Return the agency to its traditional mission of setting standards.	854.7	246	608.7
International Trade Admin.		Most of this agency is involved in providing subsidies to businesses, which can take care of themselves, and promoting industrial policy. These functions should be eliminated. Remainder of ITA, which enforces "unfair" trade laws, should be combined with a scaled-down Export Administration Office and transferred to Treasury Dept.	266.5	40	226.5
Nat'l. Oceanic & Atmos. Admin.		Some of this agency's functions can be privatized, i.e., portions of the functions of the National Weather Service. Funds for the National Marine Fisheries, subsidizing the fishing industry, can also be reduced.	1829	1523	306

Account	Policy	Policy Rationale	1995	Proposed Funding	Savings
		DEPARTMENT OF JUSTICE			
Violent Crime Reduction Trust Fund Crime Prevention	Terminate	This is a grab-bag of liberal social programs, not a crime reduction package.	103.5	0	103.5
Office of Justice Programs Juvenile Justice Programs		This program has no track record of success. States, if they wish, can fund these programs from their block grant money.	155.3	0	155.3
		DEPARTMENT OF TRANSPORTATION			
Maritime Administration	Terminate Bureau, transferring funds for ready reserve force to Defense Department	Subsidies to Maritime Industry contradict a free trade policy. Graduates of the State Maritime Institutions are no longer needed for national defense. Industry specific research and development should be a private sector responsibility. Termination of guaranteed loan subsidy is consistent with the movement to market based criteria for loans.	340	150	190
Federal Transit Admin.		Studies have consistantly shown that Federal investment in new mass transit facilities is highly questionable; ridership levels fail to meet projections.	4614.3	0	4614.3
		Subsidies allow states to invest in these non-cost effective projects. They should be terminated and mass transit agencies should charge prices that reflect true cost.			

Account	Policy	Policy Rationale	1995	Proposed Funding	Savings
		DEPARTMENT OF DEFENSE			
Corps of Engineers General Investigations	Cut 30%	Refocus the Corps of Engineers' role to consist of providing flood control projects, and economic projects that are multi-state sponsored and provide national benefits. Eliminate the Corps role in local projects and all recreational projects, as well as eliminating followup maintanence of already existing state recreational facilities. Fund future projects with positive current benefit to current cost ratios. Implement user fees on all existing Federal non-flood control projects.	3236	2265.2	970.7
		DEPARTMENT OF EDUCATION			
Impact Aid	Terminate	States use these funds to offset the cost of providing education to dependents of Federal & military workers in their state. However, these Federal and military workers provide benefits to the community, something the communities recognize, or else they would not fight so hard to keep them. This program allows states the luxury of receiving the extra benefits at lower cost.	728	0	728
Howard Univ.	Terminate	Howard University has a wealthy, prestigious alumni, it should start an endowment like any other university.	206.5	0	206.5

Account	Policy	Policy Rationale	1995	Proposed Funding	Savings
		DEPARTMENT OF HEALTH & HUMAN SERVICES			
Health Curriculum Assistance		This is a subsidy for future upper income people.	288.7	0	288.7
Refugee & Entrant Assist.	Cut 50%	Provide assistance to needy refugee children only.	406	203	203
Nat'l. Inst. of Health	Cut 200 million	Eliminate excess overhead paid to colleges and universities.			200
Agency for Health Care Policy & Research	Terminate	Originally mandated to collect statistics and do research, this bureau has increasingly assumed an advocacy role. Other departments can assume its original responsibilities.	138.6	0	138.6
Indian Health Services	Terminate Cut to 1988 inflation adjusted level.	Department has experienced explosive growth in last seven years, partially contributing to the department's mismanagement. Cuts in funding will force it to prioritize. Health care policy changes, such as increasing the use of managed care, will decrease health care related expenses.	1967	1317.6	649.1

DEPARTMENT OF HOUSING & URBAN DEVELOPMENT
This Dep't. will be terminated, its remaining duties transferred to Office of Housing Programs

Account	Policy	Policy Rationale	1995	Proposed Funding	Savings
Community Planning & Development		The Community Development block grant is discussed in Chapter 5. The remainder of this bureau funds strictly local programs, and states can choose to fund them, if they believe they are an efficient use of funds. Oth-			

Account	Policy	Policy Rationale	1995	Proposed Funding	Savings
		erwise, restrictions on the amount of Federal money flowing to local areas and projects may encourage states and localities to review the programs they fund, with an eye towards determing those that are necessary and those that are luxuries. Less funding may encourage states to find better, more efficient solutions to the problems they believe they are confronting.	2593	0	2593

DEPARTMENT OF VETERANS AFFAIRS

Account	Policy	Policy Rationale	1995	Proposed Funding	Savings
Construction Construction, Major	Eliminate new construction.	More construction would add to the surplus of hospital beds that exist in many of the communities where the VA intends to build hospitals. Further, eliminating funds for new construction should force the VA to establish a cost efficient modernization plan.	355	55	300
Construction, Minor	Cut 10%	VA contracting practices are notoriously inefficient.	153.5	138.15	15.35
Departmental Admin. Gen'l. Operating Expenses	Cut 10%	Department is notoriously overstaffed and inefficiently managed. A restriction of general operating funds should encourage them to manage more cost effectively, or else curtail operations significantly.	890	801	89

Account	Policy	Policy Rationale	1995	Proposed Funding	Savings
		DEPARTMENT OF INTERIOR			
Bureau of Mines Mines & Minerals	Terminate, transferring 30 million to Bureau of Land Mgmt. for basic research.	Most of this bureau's original functions have been taken over by other agencies. The remaining functions, such as gathering data for public dissemination and conducting research on mining techniques, can be handled by private companies.	152.7	30	122.7
U.S. Geological Survey Surveys, Invest. & Research	Terminate	Many alternative institutions, both private and governmental, are capable of providing the services, such as mapping and environmental studies, provided by Geological survey. Other programs, such as the federal-state cooperative program of water division, will be eliminated.	572.6	0	572.6
Fish & Wildlife & Parks National Biological Survey Res., Inv. & Svys.	Terminate	This program has not been authorized and is still searching for a mission.	167.2	0	167.2
National Park Service Land Acquisition	Terminate	Govt. owns enough land and should not buy more. Mgmt. of existing inventory shifted to operating accounts. The rest of the Service has increased rapidly, with an emphasis on environmental concerns, applied without adequate consideration of benefits and costs.	1434	1090	344

Account	Policy	Policy Rationale	1995	Proposed Funding	Savings
U.S. Fish & Wildlife Svc. Land Acquisition	Terminate	Govt. owns enough land. Mgmt. of existing inventory shifted to operating accounts.	67.4	0	67.4
Resource Mgmt.	Cut to 1988 inflation adjusted level.	These accounts are a few of the many accounts that have increased rapidly, with an emphasis on environmental concerns, applied in a heavy-handed fashion.	512.8	448.8	64
Construction	Cut to 1988 inflation adjusted level.		53.9	32.9	21
Land & Minerals Mgmt. Minerals Mgmt. Svc. *Royalty & Offshore Minerals*	Cut 50 %	Sell future royalty streams of federal offshore leases, avoiding the expenses associated with collecting them. Close Outer Continental Shelf regional offices, (except New Orleans) in light of the greatly reduced Outer Continental Shelf leasing.	189.1	94.55	94.55
Bureau of Indian Affairs	Cut to 1988 inflation adjusted level.	Recent criticism suggests that the Department is extremely mismanaged, partially as a result of large growth in recent years. Department should be scaled back, & forced to prioritize programs rather than proceed in a helter-skelter fashion.	1657	1380.7	276.3

		INDEPENDENT AGENCIES			
Small Business Admin. *	Terminate	Termination is consistent with movement to market based criteria for loans. Much of the assistance of			

* Because the loan programs were funded substantially from unobligated balances in 1995, a greater amount would be required to fund these programs in 1996 and beyond.

Account	Policy	Policy Rationale	1995	Proposed Funding	Savings
		this agency is targeted to special interest groups, e.g. minority ownership. Some of the funds go to subsidize retired businessman. Advocacy programs will continue to be funded, 8.2 million being merged with funds in the Min. Bus. Dev. Agency and transferred to Commerce & Labor.	814	8.2	805.8
Legal Services Corp.	Terminate	This agency has mush-roomed into a $400 million corporation, that, far from concentrating on its original mission of meeting high priority legal needs of the poor, has extended itself all across the U.S., funding liberal political advocacy groups. States can fund this program from their block grant funds if they wish.	415	0	415
Appalachian Reg'l Comm.	Terminate	Funds local development projects, which are both duplicative of other programs and have not been shown to be effective.	282	0	282
Tennessee Valley Auth.	Make self supporting.	Costs of maintaining TVA's power system should be borne by users of its power. Many of TVA's other activities, such as providing recreational facilities, are local in nature and should not be federally funded.	142.9	0	142.9
Railroad Retirement Board Dual Benefits Payments	Terminate	Simply an additional payment to Railroad Workers, above Social Security benefits. Approximately $ 1000 per rail employee.	261	0	261

Account	Policy	Policy Rationale	1995	Proposed Funding	Savings
Payments to Postal Service	Terminate	Postal Service should fund itself with receipts from stamp revenue.	92.3	0	92.3
General Services Administration Federal Buildings Fund	Rescind Unobligated Balance, Cut balance by 20%.	In 1995, GSA plans to obligate 8.5 billion for payments. Because we are eliminating Departments and reducing FTE's, the government should be in a position to sell space, not rent. We will rescind 2.6 billion in unobligated balances, and reduce the remaining 5.9 billion by 20%. This produces a savings of 3.8 billion below 1995 level. These savings can be realized by not reducing the funds appropriated for other government agencies for transfer to GSA, and, when those funds are transferred to GSA, either rescinding them or lowering the amount that can be obligated each year. Alternatively, each agency budget which includes an amount for transfer to this account could be reduced.			3780
Interstate Commerce Comm.	Terminate	Continuation of motor carrier industry is an inefficient use of tax dollars. For example, ICC regulates entry of motor carriers, yet over 95% of applications are approved. ICC also regulates rail abandonments, yet there are few, if any. Antitrust and consumer protection activities can be transferred to FTC or DOJ, within their existing budgets	33	0	33

Account	Policy	Policy Rationale	1995	Proposed Funding	Savings

CORPORATION FOR NATIONAL & COMMUNITY SERVICE

Account	Policy	Policy Rationale	1995	Proposed Funding	Savings
Nat'l & Community Svc.	Terminate	This is a new program. It should be terminated because the gov't. should not pay people to volunteer.	575	0	575

ENVIRONMENTAL PROTECTION AGENCY

Account	Policy	Policy Rationale	1995	Proposed Funding	Savings
Research & Devel.	Cut to 1988 inflation adjusted level.	Many of EPA's program accounts are duplicative of activities in other accounts. Also, many of EPA's research is duplicative of research conducted by other Departments, such as Interior and Agriculture. Significant savings can result from eliminating this duplication. Further, some of the Agency's activities, such as the Environmental Technology Initiative, focus on applied research and product development. Government agencies should not be involved in commercial research and development programs.	350	244.2	105.8
Haz. Substance Superfund *(Includes funds for Payment to Hazardous Substance Superfund)*	Cut 20%	This program should be restructered significantly. The EPA should be required to use the expertise of the Corps of Engineers and Bureau of Reclamation to implement Superfund cleanup and construction. The agency should choose cleanup standards so that they are consistent with the use of the land. As responsibility for the superfund cleanup devolves to states, Federal oversight funds should be			

Account	Policy	Policy Rationale	1995	Proposed Funding	Savings
		significantly reduced; the states are perfectly capable of implementing these programs.	1685	1348	337

NATIONAL AERONAUTICS & SPACE ADMINISTATION (NASA)

Account	Policy	Policy Rationale	1995	Proposed Funding	Savings
Human Space Flight Space Station *(OMB estimate, includes funds appropriated for space station in NASA R&D account)*	Privatize	The creation of the Space Station has been justified on 2 bases; 1. experimentation in the life sciences and 2. development of commercial activities such as medicine, in near-zero gravity. The first purpose can be accomplished in cooperation with the Russian Space Station MIR. If the second purpose does indeed have commercial value, it should be funded with private capital.	2121	0	2121
Space Shuttle	Privatize	Private firms can provide shuttle services cheaper and more efficiently. NASA however, will continue to train astronauts. (Calculation assumes 15% savings.)	2993	2544	449
Human Space Flight US/Russian Coop. Prog.	Cut 10%	Privatization of Space Station and Space shuttle should allow for significant cuts	142.6	128.34	14.26
Payload & Utilization	Cut 20%		304	243.2	60.8
Science, Aeronautics & Technology	Terminate Academic Programs.	No need to introduce NASA space flight programs to elementary and secondary education students in the age of Cable TV. No evidence such programs are effective in			

Account	Policy	Policy Rationale	1995	Proposed Funding	Savings
		increasing student interest in science. Further, this program is another example of Federal involvement in education, with a significant portion set aside for minority students. States can use their block grant funds to promote such education if they choose to.	97	0	97
	Cut 5% after terminating academic programs.	NASA programs have repeatedly been criticized as plagued by poor contracting and oversight practices. Cuts are not deeper however, because, in conjunction with the privatization of the space station and the space shuttle, NASA's budget should more accurately reflect a greater emphasis on space science, an area where it has had its greatest consistent success.	5804	5513.8	290.2
Mission Support Research & Program Mgmt.	Cut 20%	Primarily a S & E account, privitization of the space station and space shuttle should allow for significant savings in this account.	2166	1732.56	433.14

NATIONAL SCIENCE FOUNDATION

Account	Policy	Policy Rationale	1995	Proposed Funding	Savings
Academic Research Infras.	Terminate	Universities should finance their own infrastructure, using either private funds or, if they choose, state grants.	250	0	250
Major Research Equipment	Terminate	Universities should finance their own infrastructure, using either private funds or, if they choose, state grants.	126	0	126

Account	Policy	Policy Rationale	1995	Proposed Funding	Savings
Educ. & Human Res.	Terminate funds for educational system reform, and EPSCoR.	These funds support curriculum development and teacher training, which are subsidies to the education lobby. EPSCoR provides funds to second tier research institutions not eligible for NSF grants, to improve their research capabilities so that they will be eligible for NSF grants.	96.8 36.9	0 0	96.8 36.9
Educ. & Human Res.	Cut remaining funds 50% and Block Grant (Educ.).	These funds support a variety of K - 12 and college education programs, many of which are of an informal, inconsistent nature. Their impact is highly questionable. These targeted funds should be cut by 50%, and passed on to the states for use.	472.2	236.1	236.1
Research & Related Act.	Cut 90 million.	Excess overhead.			90

APPENDIX

Congress of the U.S.		We would cut the Congress' budget by 15% through reduction of committee staff, reduction of support organizations, which often duplicate one another, restraining free mail, and reducing benefits such as pensions.	2367	2012	355
Repeal the Davis-Bacon Act		This act requires that "prevailing wages" be paid on all federally-assisted construction projects above $2,000. As a result the federal government pays more than it would under competitive bidding. (The savings estimate includes			

Account	Policy	Policy Rationale	1995	Proposed Funding	Savings
		defense amounts.)	390	0	390
Modify the Service Contract Act		This act also raises government outlays by setting labor standards above those that would exist in a competitive market. (Again, the savings estimate includes defense amounts.)	200	0	200
Across the Board Cuts		On most amounts for which we did not suggest a specific program charge we reduce spending five percent below the 1995 level. Given the large increase since 1988 in domestic discretionary spending, these accounts can easily absorb this reduction.			2831

The Progress & Freedom Foundation

The Progress & Freedom Foundation is dedicated to creating a positive vision of the future founded in the historic principles of the American Ideal. A non-partisan research and educational organization under section 501[C](3) of the IRS Code, it is supported by tax deductible contributions from foundations, individuals and corporations.

For more information about the Progress & Freedom Foundation, contact

The Progress & Freedom Foundation
1250 H Street NW
Washington, DC 20005
Voice: 202/484-2312
Facsimile: 202/484-9326
E-Mail: PFF@aol.com